I0570242

TORTOISE TREKKER ADVENTURES

TORTOISE TREKKER
ADVENTURES

RAMBLINGS IN THE WHITE MOUNTAINS AND BEYOND

ABBIE JO GLEESON

PALMETTO

PUBLISHING

Charleston, SC
www.PalmettoPublishing.com

© 2024 Abbie Jo Wojtowicz
All rights reserved.
No portion of this book may be reproduced,
stored in a retrieval system, or transmitted in
any form by any means—electronic, mechanical,
photocopy, recording, or other—except for
brief quotations in printed reviews,
without prior permission of the author.

Paperback ISBN: 979-8-9911781-0-5

To Nancy – my inspiration and friend!

ACKNOWLEDGMENTS

This is possibly the hardest part of writing this book. Where to start and stop? I could very well write a whole book of acknowledgments. There are just soooo many people to thank so I'm sure to miss quite a few someones. With that said, I'll do my best to articulate my gratitude to everyone that inspired, supported, laughed with and at me.

The idea of this book was born after a post hike write-up on Facebook went viral. Okay, not viral, but it did get a great response. Initially, I kept a journal in my usual nerdy way with miles, elevation gain, time on the trail. As I started posting my post-hike write-ups I sprinkled my own quirky and unique observations on the challenges of hiking up mountains. Like, how much things ached, how often I stumbled and fell, while laughing at myself through my misery. Then I realized my observations weren't quite so unique and that my antics seemed to resonate with others.

There were (are) so many hiking buddies that I found through the Hiking Buddies NH48 group on Facebook. What an amazing community! It was through this group that I made friends other turtle hikers. We may not be trail runners but we have each other's backs, okay sometimes we're on our backs, but we make sure no one is left behind.

Though you dudes are important it has been my hiking sisters that really inspire and motivate me. It has been my hiking sisters that have encouraged me, not only on so many adventures, but also to compile these stories and publish this book. Creating a list of all these amazing women is hard because I know I'll forget someone but here it goes. My heartfelt appreciation to Nancy Hall, Suzzy Deets, Michele, Lisa, Michele, Stacy, Cheryl, Jennifer, Jo-Ann, Nancy, Kimberly, Marie, MJ, Eurydice, Christina, Judy, Joanna, Julie, Malia, Cathy, Kathleen, Lynn, Lori, Kathy, Vicky, Laura, Amy, Kim, Jenn, Christine, Debra, Julie, Alicia, Aerin, Sandra, Laurie, Novlette, Laurie, Beth, Georgann, Eugenia, Sierra, and Dominique.

Special thanks to The Mountain Wanderer himself, Steve Smith, for never tiring of answering all my questions. I stopped into the bookstore in Lincoln whenever I was passing through. There were many times where he could have just directed me to one of his written guides, which I love and reference anyways, but instead he was always willing to chat. I often asked about what current conditions might be like. I am very grateful and honored that you took the time to read through the book and edited what must have sounded like rambling. I appreciate your encouragement and providing me hope that others might enjoy my adventures.

There are so many others who have continued to support me through all my craziness. Your love and support helped me decide to take a leap of faith, quit my job (conveniently called it retirement), hiked A LOT, and move so I could continue my love affair with The White Mountains. This includes, but not limited to, Tami Jean, Teresa, Nell, Pat, Edie, The Thursday Night Dinner Crew, former partners, family and FB followers.

To my mountain man, Dave Estes, who I'm grateful for finding because I did take that leap of faith. Your support, constant reading of my never ending edits, and willingness to help me get ready at 4:00 am to head out on more adventures is so very much appreciated.

Thank you to my son Peter, who received Garmin links at all hours of the morning to track his crazy mother, much to his dismay.

Others who have inspired me are those that have published about first hand experiences about hiking. Thanks to Ken Bosse for sharing his publishing experience. Special thanks to Erik Hamilton for providing several self-publishing options and the experience he had publishing "The Other 52..."

Thanks to everyone that works on creating and maintaining trails in all the wild places for the public to enjoy and by amazed by being out in nature. This includes those working for independent land trusts as well as Nationally Reserved Lands. Thanks to AMC trail workers for your hard work in maintaining the trails for us incline addicts.

I'm especially in awe of those that volunteer as Search and Rescue Personnel. Many thanks to New Hampshire Fish and Game, who organize all of the search, rescue, and recovery efforts in the New Hampshire White Mountains. There are many local groups that work diligently to ensure missing and/or injured hikers return home safely, whenever possible.

DISCLAIMER

This book is based on the author's experiences and not meant as a guide. The author's opinions are strictly their own and not reflective of any other individuals or institutions. Some names have been changed for individuals privacy.

INTRODUCTION

Welcome to a Tortoise Hiker's obsession with the White Mountains and other remote places.

It was by chance that I started an obsession and full out love affair with the White Mountains of New Hampshire. In the following pages, please find some hope that, no matter who you are or what your background, you may have your own adventures and take flight in fulfilling your dream. Even if you don't know what that dream is.

This is not intended as a guidebook, though there is a section with a list of resources for preparing and enjoying your adventures in the areas that I write about. Preparing can be its own reward and its own adventure.

Why and how does one get hooked on The 48 – 4000 Footer List? The reasons, I think, are as individual as snowflakes. Honestly, mine has changed and I'm sure will again before I'm done. All I can really tell you is my story. As I started to compile my accounts through the White Mountains, I realized that, well, the answer is, I don't think I have a great answer. I was a little over half-way through the 48 list and well on my way into the 52 With A View (52WAV) list and other lists I have inadvertently started but don't know enough to track yet when I decided to compile the stories within.

Before we dive in I must talk about the hiking community. To say that this is a fellowship is a gross understatement. There are folks from every walk of life joined together by our shared passion. It is not possible for me to share my stories without also sharing some of them and theirs. Won't you join me and my trail family (tramily) on our journey?

FROM CHILDHOOD

I'm originally from Central New York where we lived out in farm country, otherwise known as the boondocks. We had our own little patch of land, complete with a freshwater pond, fields that we rented to local farmers, and a few acres of woodlands. This is where my love of the great outdoors began. It helped that I had two brothers that were boy scouts and we all learned outdoorsmanship during campouts, since it was very much a family affair.

When going out into the woods on my own, I found the best spot hang out was on a perch provided by a giant root that formed itself into a seat at the base of my favorite tree. It was set on a hillside and provided a perfect place to watch the beaver work cutting down trees and building a magnificent fort. Their tireless work was inspiring. Perhaps this was when I decided that I too wanted to build magnificent structures helped my transformation into an engineer. This was a secret place was where I'd seek refuge every chance I could. I imagined being whatever and whoever, wherever I desired. Many days I'd go there just to daydream. It was a place I could rest my soul, for I was a very old young person.

I'd learned how to build a fire thanks to the boy scouts outings. The best fires were built in the woods and I'd made myself a small firepit near my perch. Sometimes I'd bring a can of soup or beans, or Dinty Moore Beef Stew, a delightful treat those days and considered a luxury item at the time, to cook in the can over an open flame.

This place is where Robert Frost Poems would come alive for me. And that I myself was first transformed from the geeky, shy, awkward girl that didn't fit in to being just myself, strong smart and complete. Time stood still, yet I was impatient to grow up and be like the beaver, build something extraordinary with their everyday tasks.

Fast forward from a wild child romping in the woods, picking blackberries, raspberries and wild flowers to a middle aged (or rather more than middle aged) woman who was a successful professional engineer and mother to an adult son. There I was, an empty nester, working woman in a job that had run through its days feeling fulfilled and reduced to the twisted tales of on-line dating fiascos that could fill a book all on their own, who seemed to be just going through the motions of the day to day survival. Until, I decided to join a couple of friends on an outing. We were to hike up to Mount Lafayette in the White Mountains of New Hampshire. I had no idea that that one decision would help change the trajectory of my life and lead me to a new, yet very familiar, lifestyle. Back to my roots but with mountains thrown in as an added bonus, well, and a bit more of a challenge. What's life without challenge? The reward seems so much sweeter when you have to work for it. Yes, I know I'm not the first one to say, think or experience that sentiment, and I surely won't be the last.

FIRST 4000 FOOTER ATTEMPT

Be careful who you go out with for a late-night snack. It all started with a gathering of friends and small talk at Margarita's one night. A friend had hiked all of the New Hampshire 4000 Footers and had made plans to stay at the Greenleaf Hut and hike up to Mount Lafayette. I decided to join in what sounded like a fun time with friends. I was pretty much blissfully ignorant of what I had gotten myself into. It sounded like a great idea at the time. The person who originally planned to go had instructed me just to go online and see if there were any bunks available at the Greenleaf Hut. I went ahead and secured my spot.

I had no idea what a 4000 Footer was or what this endeavor meant. This was sometime in summer of 2017, long before I started logging my hikes or even knew there was this "List". We left from Connecticut in late morning and arrived at the Greenleaf Trailhead early afternoon.

As we arrived at the trailhead and were putting on our packs we talked to a couple of people that looked like they had refrigerators strapped to their backs. One was a young woman who was carrying at least as much weight as she was herself. We were in awe and found out they were part of the Greenleaf Hut croo. That's when I learned that the items for the Hut had to be hand carried in and it was on the backs of these inspiring young people.

Prior to the trip I had looked online as to what might be needed. Though I had done many outdoor activities growing up and when my son, Peter, was in boy scouts, all of our hikes were day hikes, and none of them were in the mountains. Any camping out overnight had parking spots so we could load as much as we needed in the car. I'd learned that the Huts had wool blankets for bedding but it was suggested that you bring a liner or lightweight sleeping bag.

Based on my investigation, I picked up a new summer sleeping bag to bring along. Knowing we'd get fed both dinner the evening we arrived and breakfast the next morning was a relief so that cut down on how much food we'd need to carry ourselves. I brought a change of clothes, some water, and not much else carried in an old school backpack that Peter didn't need any longer. My hiking boots at that time were Sketchers, nice leather, heavy soles and not much in the way of ankle support but they seemed sturdy enough. I had trekking poles so decided to use them.

Ignorance continued to be bliss and we headed into the woods. The croo member was out of sight before we actually stepped onto the trail. It was quite a while ago, so my memory doesn't serve me so well but I was just shy of 50, and though I'd run marathons, and was even training for my second Ragnar (a 2,000 mile relay race), the hike up to the hut quite literally kicked my butt.

I dare say that hiking a mountain in the Whites is actually con-sidered climbing a mountain. For in order to summit, while not nec-essarily technically challenging, one must put in much effort into going up. That effort includes preparation before, endurance during, and calm reverie after said hike.

We arrived at the hut just in time for dinner. And by just in time, I mean that everyone else was already seated so we found a couple open seats and the food started being passed around. After dinner there was a talk outside on the back deck where we could clearly see the ridge and Mount Lafayette beyond. The discussion gave an education on the different environmental areas of the mountains. We had the chance to speak with some of the other AMC members and trail stewards afterwards. That's when I first learned of the 10 essentials. These are items that one should carry with you whenever exploring in remote and wild places. These are listed in many of the Appalachian Mountain Club (AMC) literature that I was introduced to on that trip including The AMC White Mountain Guide. I was missing a few of these items. One of the items was a whistle of course they had them available at the hut, so I bought one and attached it to my pack. I also bought a pair of gloves because even though it was summer the temperatures had dipped close to freezing.

The AMC trail service member regaled us with the story of Guy Waterman, who decided to hike up voluntarily and sit atop Mount Lafayette one February and stay there.

The story included how Guy was a volunteer trail maintenance worker for many years, working upon the Franconia Ridge. The person telling the story said how Guy had left a suicide note and that several of his friends went after him. They found him the next day, his body covered in snow. Though they were baffled by the why of it. It was suggested that the mountain be named after him. Others disagreed, saying that it would go against his own principles. Which, I later found out, were documented in a book, "Backwoods Ethics," written by him and his wife Laura. The popular Leave No Trace (LNT) movement could very well be attributed to that book, where they suggested leaving only footprints in the woods.

I was both enchanted and haunted by the tale of Guy Waterman.

It was time to turn in and I had chosen a bed above my friend. He'd warned that he sometimes talked in his sleep. He was true to his word, but not only did he talk, he sang and laughed as well. I found it amusing and somewhat delightful, not sure that everyone did. So, if you plan on staying at a hut overnight, I'd recommend earplugs.

The next morning we would get the weather report from the croo and it wasn't good. The report called for winds, rain, and most importantly a concern for lightning up on the open ridge. We decided to just head back down. We chose The Old Bridle Path for our descent. It rained the whole time we hiked and it was pretty much like walking in a stream. It was just as hard going down as it had been going up.

Following are some take aways from my first White Mountain adventure. The boots I had might be fine for Connecticut hiking, but were damn slippery on wet stuff, and my ankles wanted more support. Temperatures were a good 20 degrees colder at or near the summit, which really surprised me that only a few thousand feet made such a difference. Especially in the summer. Never interrupt a talker, since my friend had been speaking for two hours straight and I tried to get a word in, caused him to snap, and well, he still hasn't forgiven me for interrupting. Trekking poles are a life saver, a cheap pair from Job Lot did the trick, and I continue to use poles to this day. Staying at an AMC hut is the bomb.

I dare say that hiking a mountain in the Whites is actually considered climbing a mountain. For in order to summit, while not necessarily technically challenging, one must put in much effort into going up. That effort includes preparation before, endurance during, and calm reverie after said hike.

MEETING MY FIRST
4000 FOOTER BUDDY
AND HIKING DOGGO

After the unsummitted Lafayette trip it was time to get busy hiking. A friend had the Blue Blaze Trail book for Connecticut and I was on a mission to hike all the trails listed. My first task was to obtain proper equipment. Eastern Mountain Sports (EMS) was definitely the place to go get outfitted at the time. Hiking pants, raincoat, first pair of smartwool socks were all purchased during round one. With knowledge of 10 essentials, I decided to that a Leatherman would be added to the mix.

I talked with someone at EMS about packs and the right kind of hiking boots. At the time EMS had knowledgeable folks on staff to focus on your needs. Depending on what you were trying to do, the employees would send you to the person with the expertise in the field you were interested in. Bob for boats, Cindy for cycles, Herb for hiking, etc… So, I tried on hiking boots and Herb gave me some things to think about. I still wasn't sure which ones I wanted but the field was beginning to narrow.

My friend Suzzy invited me to join a Hiking with Doggos group even though I didn't have a dog at the time. Every couple of weeks I'd hike with the Hiking with Doggos and join as the without-a-Doggo person. When Suzzy was there, I would borrow her goofy pup, Freya. It was a perfect fit, since I can be a bit goofy myself from then on I become Freya's Auntie. I enjoyed the rapturous ruckus of the hounds. Free to come and go, blissfully bounding to and fro. I learned to take enough food for myself and snacks for Doggos, which was a risky business. Eventually, I learned how to give out snacks without causing mass hysteria.

The very best part of Hiking with Doggos without-a-Doggo was that I got to play with all the pups, spoil them with treats, then let them go back home with someone else. I was not in a position to take on the responsibility of having my own pup. I didn't want to leave a dog at home by themselves while I was at work all day, or leave them alone for days, or board them at a kennel when the whim to travel came upon me. I was foot loose and fancy free, so to speak, without someone else to depend on me for the time being.

However, it did come up during those hikes that one of the women worked for a rescue. She stated that sometimes people needed a temporary foster, like when they would go on vacation or travel for work. I expressed interest in a short-term gig, since that seemed like it was right up my alley.

I know, I know, you're probably thinking, "what the hell does this have to do with hiking?"

If you bear with me, I promise, it will take us back to hiking.

So, said woman and I exchanged contact info. The following week I get a text staying that there's a dog in need and that they just saved it. It needed immediate foster care. She wanted to know if she could come out and inspect the house to see if it was suitable. I think they are more stringent for animal foster than for human fosters, but that's a whole other can of worms. It was determined that I, and my home, were "fit" for fostering an emergency rescue dog.

The initial report I received about the dog in need was that the vet who was asked to put the dog to sleep stepped in and saved him. All I was told in the beginning was that it was an older Havanese with some behavioral issues.

The woman who had adopted him brought him in to be euthanized and that's when the vet stepped in. Let's just say that there was way more to reveal than what the rescue people disclosed in the beginning. I was told that they wanted me to take him in so he could decompress and be evaluated. I agreed, with the condition that it was temporary. I emphasized "temporary" and reiterated the fact that I wasn't home enough to care for an animal, especially if it had special needs. I agreed to two months, three at the most. It was late February.

The rescue people made it sound like the adopter was an older woman who just didn't want to deal with him. My contact said that the dog, Jeter, had some possessive and nervous issues. Jeter was on a daily dose of Xanax and as needed basis of sedatives. Well, all of that was to put it mildly. He'd been left alone for several years in an abandoned house, but I didn't find out that information until later.

The first night Jeter was with me he paced and cried and barked and whined, all night long. Even with the sedative. I think that the Xanax actually seemed to make him more paranoid, but long story even longer, it turned into several months and me getting bitten more times than I can tell you. Not nips, he was trying to tear pieces of flesh off of my hand. Even with double gloved hands, he would bite through and get me bleeding.

The first week or so that I had Jeter, I met a woman who was the President of Groton Open Space Association (GOSA). GOSA is an organization that owns and manages land trusts to keep wild places undeveloped in Connecticut. She asked me to join one of their hikes and then trail maintenance activity. I showed up at the trail maintenance event. How fun it was to be involved with actually creating a hiking trail. The area we were working in had been cleared to create a Rabbitat (habitat for rabbits), this one was specifically created for the New England cottontail. There was hoeing, raking, mowing, moving rocks and logs, and clearing an area for walking.

I was sent down to an area to clear. As I was weeding and hoeing up walked a man who said, "I was told that you could use some help over here."

I looked up and recognized his face and surprised myself by asking "didn't you just retire?"

I must have seen a flyer at work, because I'd never formally met him before. We hit it off famously. We shared contact information and I let him know about the Facebook group Outdoor Doggos. Dick brought his dog Sport to the next doggo hike. Sport was a huge hit! Dick was an awesome Doggo Dad to boot.

At one point during the doggo hike, we came across a deer skeleton hanging in a tree. Sport kept jumping up until he got ahold of it and played tug of war until he finally brought down a leg and part of the spine. Of course, while he was jumping up, not to be deterred, the other doggo parents did not share Dick's acceptance of letting their pups partake in the scavenge. Instead, many were screeching, hollering, and grabbing their dogs giving that "oh, that's disgusting" with "that" tone in their voices.

You never saw a prouder dog than Sport with his prized thigh bone and spine still attached. He was allowed to bring it home as a reward for a day well spent on the trail. I fell in love with that dog right then and there. Sport was truly a Dog's Dog.

Right after that hike, I ditched the sketcher boots, or rather turned them into my working in the yard boots and bought my first pair of Merrell's. I decided to go to Bobs Store, where I normally get my running shoes and was excited that they were having an Everything in the Store 20% Sale. Yeah, you guessed it, except for Merrell's. The old bait and switch, but I bit the bullet and paid full price because my feet, ankles, legs, and back are worth it.

Fitted with my new shoes, I wanted to take them for a spin. I hadn't brought Jeter to any of the doggo hikes yet because I wasn't sure how he'd react to the other doggos. Dick offered to have Sport provide us with a test hike. Sport was a good sport, or as Dick likes to say, Sport was a real Sport. He wasn't bothered by Jeter a bit. I felt confident enough to start bringing Jeter on the Doggo hikes.

As far as Jeter was concerned, I was patient, and kind, and loving. Also, I had a job to go to and as I kept telling the rescue folks that I wasn't around to give him constant care. He did enjoy going outside, and the hiking with the doggos became a highlight of the week, for both of us. Jeter was a little spitfire and threw his 18 pounds around, or rather carried his 18 pound self with a lot of arrogance letting all the "big dogs" know that he was "THE Big Dog". Well, except for when we came to water crossings, then he'd come up to me to pick him up and carry him over. I obliged.

When Jeter was getting his way, he was a real cutie pie and love bug. However, he was so psychologically damaged, that I'm not sure anyone could have completely helped ease his suffering. As soon as it started to get dark, the night terrors would haunt him. No amount of holding, cajoling, comforting, or even sedation would dispel them. He would go into a trance each night and become frantic. Come morning his anxiety would be sky high, and trying to calm him enough for his daily dose of Xanax was met with his total displeasure.

After four months I started providing weekly reports and asking if they found a forever home yet. It became clear that they wanted me to keep him. I still could not and as a matter of fact would be heading out of town in a few months. I did the best I could during that time to give him a good life for as long as I was able. It came out that the woman who had adopted Jeter had let the rescue people know of his afflictions. Just like me, they ignored her concerns.

The next couple of months were spent walking in the woods in Connecticut. Sunday mornings with the Doggos and a couple times a week with Dick and Sport. During that time Dick sold his rental house on the Cape and searched for a new rental property in New Hampshire. That's when The White Mountain Fever hit us both and whilst looking at his next vacation home location we started Hiking!

FIRST TWO 4000 FOOTERS

Dick and I took a few days and took a trip to New Hampshire where we looked at real estate for prospective rental property. Naturally, we took the opportunity to hike while we were there. We left the doggos in Connecticut. It was just five days shy of my 52nd Birthday when we hiked up Mount Jackson by the Jackson-Webster Trail. It was amazing, even without the views since it was socked in. Okay, back then I used the term cloudy, "socked in" was one of those terms I will come to appreciate later.

I can still remember that even though it was overcast, the lure of hiking in them thar woods brought on an enchantment. The higher up, the smell of the balsam added to the misty glow and at any moment I believed a woodland fairy, nymph, or other such mystical creature could let their presence be known and it would not be a surprise.

Though I've spent much time in the woods, this was a much more transcendental experience. As we hiked into the boreal forest a sense of the past surrounded us. Where giants, unicorns, and sprites make their home. The scent of balsam fills your nostrils while the spirit of the imagination fills your mind. Of course, that was disturbed by the scrambling up to the summit. Though having no views was a bit of a disappointment, the experience was what drew me in.

We scrambled and butt slid back down the scrambly section. Dick stopped, took out some trail mix, and held out his hand. It was my first experience with the Gray Jays of The White Mountains. I was mesmerized as this beautiful creature swooped in, landed long enough to grab a treat and off again.

Then it was my turn. As I put a couple pieces of the treats in my palm, I filled with excitement. Like an electric charge that goes through your body right before a lightning storm happens, not that I've been struck by lightning. It happened so quickly, yet also as if in slow motion. The gray jay dropped in and found its treat and was swooping back away. And yes, that's when I knew that magic happens in The Whites.

On our way back down the mountain we could see the sun's rays starting to poke through the trees. We stopped and sat on Bugle Cliff as the sky opened up and we were treated to amazing vistas. That was most likely the moment I fell head over heels for the White Mountains of New Hampshire with my first 4000 Footer under my belt. There was no going back. I wanted to hike ALL the mountains, especially the 48 – 4000 Footers.

The next morning, we were off to tackle Jefferson. If one 4000 Footer was good, then two should have been divine, or so I thought. Wrong! OMG! So many rock and ledge scrambles. I thought there were rock scrambles on Jackson, but they weren't even close to the nightmare that was the Caps Ridge Trail. Where each of the Caps was a rocky outcrop that felt like climbing a mini mountain all on its own.

My only consolation at the time was that Dick kept apologizing saying, "I didn't think it would be this bad."

The lower part of the trail was invigorating. The smell of the balsam was refreshing and actually encouraging. The upper part was VERY HARD, at least for me. And for this to be my second 4000 Footer was kind of crazy. We went from one of the "easiest" 4000 Footers the day before, to one of the most difficult. I'm going to say Jefferson is probably in the top five hardest list anyway.

The views were spectacular. We lucked out, thanks to how slow I was going, the clouds opened up by the time we got to the top. A lot of people before us didn't get any views.

How slow is slow? Let's put it in perspective. The day before, on Jackson we had gone 5.6 miles in 5 hours with an elevation gain of 2,418 feet. Jefferson was a total of 5.3 miles with an elevation gain of 2,708 feet. Comparable one would think, but it took us 8 hours.

Perhaps because at the bottom of each rocky outcropping I'd stand at the bottom, look up and in my head yell, loud, long and drawn out, "F####@@@@&&&&!"

I watched with envy as everyone that passed us did so with ease. Dick himself had no problem navigating these areas and would help me look for any way that afforded me SOMETHING to hang on to. Often, going way off the marked blaze marks that were painted right there on the center of a slab.

At no time did I consider getting back down, for each one of the Caps or scramble ridges tested my resolve and it was scary enough fighting gravity. Of course, Dick would bound up each one. I'm still convinced that he is part mountain goat.

I was thankful for his patience and kindness, for there was never a time where he seemed short with me even though he could often go up and down several times over as I meticulously plotted my route. He more looked at me like a curiosity at my stop and gawk moments. I was paralyzed at each and every single one we came to. These rocky slabs looked like towers to me. And I had no idea how the hell I would get up. Then he asked "what do you think when you're look-ing up at one of THESE?" as he pointed at one of the seemingly im-possible routes in front of us. Well, seeming impossible to me, that is. We were approaching the third one when he asked what I thought.

After telling him what went through my mind, he started saying "F####@@@@&&&&!" for me when we reached such areas. That was endearing.

We successfully got over all the ledges and the Caps we came to the final challenging section to summit. A dump heap of rock blocks. As if God was like a child and got tired of playing with his Legos. Then decided just to dump out his bucket of toys and let them lie where they may. Off we were to navigate the jagged lichen covered boulders. Not really scramble, but more twisty, turny on the foot and ankle. Causing one to be aware of each and every step. Now it was the mine field of rocky terrain that caused us to focus on just making it from cairn, a pile of rocks that helps mark the trail to show you the way, to cairn.

I felt as if we'd stepped onto another planet devoid of life as we know it. Mars perhaps, where everything took on the same color, not exactly a black and white film but more of a gray with greenish hew as far as the eye could see. The starkness held its own beauty and once we finally reached the summit the cairn that marked the peak was large enough to feel like we were climbing the pyramids of Egypt.

There were a couple of young men sitting at the summit when we approached. They had just come from Adams and were headed towards Washington, which I could not even imagine doing (I still can't). We took pictures of/for them and vice versa. We made our way over to another "bump" which I wasn't even sure I could get up. I was grateful that Dick was persuasive because the view from there was even more spectacular than the actual summit. My much-needed PBJ never tasted so heavenly.

Only then did I dare think about the "how the hell are we getting back down?"

Dick was worried about whether I had enough in the tank to get back down. He confessed that I wasn't looking so good on the approach to the summit. Especially after reaching the false summit. Apparently my face said it all. It was true that I was feeling pretty discouraged and disheartened at that point.

Everything changed after taking in nourishment. It's amazing that that little act can change so much. The light came back to my eye, and I was ready to go. Dick found a by-pass for the first Cap. While we were following the by-pass path it was pretty evident that though it was softer terrain, we were still atop the boulder mess. The concern was now that we didn't have visibility to the crevasses and well, slipping through the vegetation into an unseen vortex didn't seem like a very good idea. One by-pass was enough and we went back on trail.

For me it was a ton of boulder and ledge butt sliding, which made Dick chuckle, so all was not lost. Just as we were coming to the end of the Rocky Road I started to rush, to get out of people's way, then down I went. I fell forward and my poles saved the day. They acted as a bridge across a large crevasse. Even facing into it I couldn't see the bottom.

And that my friends is why I never travel without my poles, they indeed saved my life, well at least my face and possible broken bones.

What a difference a day makes. When we got to the car I declared, "I would never hike another 4000 Footer!"

WEEK OF THE PALINDROME

Our next adventure took us to the West Coast. We were going to attend my nephew's wedding in Seattle, this afforded us the opportunity to do some exploring. We planned to visit the Olympic National Park before the wedding. We'd then return to Seattle for the wedding and finish our time at Mount Rainier before heading home. Ah, but getting there was the real adventure and ne'er one to be forgotten.

Before heading out West, the Jeter story continued. Six weeks of decompression and evaluation had turned into six months of me advocating for a more stable environment for the little troubled soul in my care. During the rest of his time with me I took Jeter out as often as possible and continued to hound, maybe a little bit of a pun intended, the rescue about rehoming him. As we approached the travel date there was still no movement on a new home for Jeter or even another foster. I ended up having to bring him back to the vet's from which he was saved. The day before catching the flight to Seattle,

Jeter and I had an emotional goodbye. I was never told of where the little fellow landed.

When we landed in Seattle we decided to drive immediately up the coast to Forks, WA. Home of "Twilight". We found a place in town to eat before going to find our rental for the next couple of nights. It was a Bar and Grill, with an emphasis on the word Bar. I chuckled when Dick ordered his hamburger medium rare. It was easy to see that this was where the locals went to drink beer. It was just a happy coincidence that they happened to serve food as well. I was pretty sure the burgers were all going to be cooked the same and Dick's medium rare was exactly like my well done burger.

There are not a lot of options for accommodations in or around the Olympic National Park. By the time we decided we were going on the trip the lodgings in the park were full. The off-site options found through AirBNB were minimal. The first place I found was deemed unacceptable by Dick because they charged a cleaning fee. We were down to choosing from two locations, both claimed to be glamping facilities. They were both listed as In-tents experience were supposed to provide tents that were set up with everything one would need to be comfortable without the feel of roughing it. We, of course, chose the cheaper option.

We tried calling our In-tents host, Michelle, after we ate to let her know we were on our way. She wasn't available and the person that answered didn't seem to know what I was talking about, just stated that Michelle wasn't there. We did have the address and plugged that into our GPS. After driving past a field of cows, that turned into a dirt road, which ended up being a VERY long driveway. There were other houses in view and we finally came to a yellow house where we pulled in. The first thing we noticed was that there was just about every type of "formerly running" mechanical equipment you could think of littering the yard. These mechanical objects included but were not limited to busses, tractors, and cars. All were in various stages of disassembly.

As we walked up to the house we passed by old refrigerators laying on their backs. Filled with some type of black liquid that gave off the stench of rotting meat. We looked at each other with a bit of trepidation and I couldn't help but wonder what type of meat could be decaying in those containers? Of course, an image of Jeffery Dahmer passed across my mind.

We stepped up onto the porch and saw the front door was ajar. We did our best to knock on the door, but it opened itself more as we did. We stood there agape as the man of the house was standing across the room hollering at us to enter. He stood on the other side of an imposing dining table cluttered with a variety of objects. He was a large man with a tee shirt boasting some derogatory statement about "My wife…"

We stated that we were there to check in. He responded with a laugh and stated, "Meeeshell, she don't tell me nothin'."

He pointed beyond the house and said "Jus' drive down there. She'll come find ya."

Once we got back in the car we did discuss going somewhere else, but there was absolutely nowhere else to go. We passed the other glamping area on our way to dinner. It looked so inviting with a little store, a place they served dinner, little cabins, tents neatly in a row, and a pool. Unfortunately, there was also a big neon sign at the entrance that was lit with NO VACANCY.

Onward we drove and as we entered the "In-Tents" area there were a couple of women stumbling along the dirt path that served as a roadway, the dirt path not the women. We rolled down the window and the women both helping each other stand looked at us dazed. They were clearly under the influence. We asked if they knew where we could find Michelle.

One woman pointed at the other. "That's her. She's Michelle. Isn't she the best?"

It was approaching dusk, so daylight was fading. Michelle pointed to the first campsite in front of us and said to wait for her there. She tromped up and poked her head into the tent, then back out and said, "give us a few minutes, the kids were supposed to get it ready for you."

She finally emerged from the tent and stated, "well, maybe you'd prefer down by the river?"

But she told us to go in and see what we thought. We entered to a more than musty smell. It was obvious that the tent and everything inside had been underwater long enough to smell itself swampy.

She indicated that three and four sites down the roadway were open and that we could take our pick. So, we hurried over to see if any of those were habitable.

We passed two sites, one with people and one that Michelle said would be occupied that evening. The third site was perched atop a drop off to the river below. It provided a great view of the river though and we went inside. At least it was dry and didn't have the smell of bullfrogs and catfish. So, we told her that would do. Daylight had all but faded by then.

There was a port-a-potty back up near the first campsite. She pointed uphill saying that there were showers and a group kitchen tent ahead. It was late and we'd had a long drive, so I headed back to hit the port-a-potty. Michelle said we could take what we needed from the first tent so I dashed in and retrieved a flashlight after using the facilities, if you can call a port-a-potty the facilities that is, then headed back to settle in.

Inside the tent that was to be our home sweet home for the next two nights was an assortment of "furniture.". We assessed our surroundings with the light from the first tent. The furnishings were what one might find left over in a yard sale. A couple of plastic tables used on an outdoors deck. A couple of chairs, one was over-stuffed and another a "fancy" folding plastic chair. The bed looked inviting until we climbed in. They had actually put a mattress atop an inflatable bed so that when we laid down you were at an angle. Luckily our head was highest, but it felt like we were going to slide down and out. Exhaustion won and the sound of the river helped lull me to sleep in spite of our predicament. However, Dick only could only imagine that the sound of the river masked the sound of someone able to come in with a chainsaw at night to cut us into little pieces.

We made it through the first night. I really need coffee first thing in the morning. We decided to head into LaPush for breakfast and start exploring. After eating at an amazing breakfast spot we got to check out the coastline. There were sea stacks and the forest came right to the beach. We enjoyed the tidal pools with their brilliant-colored coral and sea anemones. We walked through the hole in the wall which was an opening in a giant rock wall. The forest ranger made sure we knew when low tide was so we didn't get stuck on the other side of the rock mass because the hole in the wall would then become inaccessible. Then, we'd have to wait there for the tide to reveal our passage back through.

Where the beach transition from forest to sandy shore there was a barrier where majestic trees had fallen trees and been bleached bone white. From the massive white logs that looked like fallen dinosaur bones transitioned to the pebbles and sandy shore leading to the pulsing ocean. What a difference from the forest lush with large trees, moss and thriving wildlife.

Later in the day, we hiked along the Hoh River, plenty of moss, ginormous trees and fresh air abound. We were transported back in time. Never had I seen trees so large. We were dwarfed by their magnificence and drawn into a carpeted green wonderland. If only we could have stayed there for the night. One of the fallen giants called to us to stay and rest. Instead, we left the comfort of the rain forest and visited the World's Largest Spruce Tree. There was a peace in being reminded of the power of nature. I was humbled and grateful for it all.

We arrived back at In-Tents in time to look around in the daylight. We saw a couple areas for showers, only one had the piping that could be attached to the water supply. We had to hook up the water line in order to get our showers. The hot water heater was not working so cold showers they were. At least we were clean and refreshed. We had time to enjoy a campfire before turning in. That was the night I was nervous because we were the only ones there. But I was more tired than afraid and zonked out as soon as my head hit the pillow.

The next morning, I decided to heat up leftovers for breakfast. We had a camp stove on site. Then, found pots, pans, and cookware in the common area kitchen mess. And I don't mean just mess like mess hall, but it was a mess. What I wanted more than anything was to make a cup of coffee. I found a container full of baskets that go in a percolator, but NO percolator container. So, improvised. Boiled water and put basket over a cup, poured boiling water over the grounds in the basket. Well, at least I had me some coffee.

Lesson learned. Pay the damn cleaning fee.

MOUNT RAINIER

Back to Seattle for the wedding. During our visit, Dick was a big hit with the family. He brought the siblings and Mom to a local brewery. The siblings and Dick discovered their drink of the night, The Raspberry Shitshow. Yup, that was the name of the beer and hence the name of the evening as it came to be known. They proceeded to indulge and tell stories of our assorted youth. I enjoyed the show while sipping seltzer.

With the newlyweds happily hitched and only minor family drama, Dick and I took our leave and headed up to Mount Rainier. I'd been to Rainier once before when Peter was young. That was a wonderful trip, so I was looking forward to returning. Our goal was to get in some hiking and get a lay of the land that first day. When we arrived at the Jackson Visitor Center in Paradise I was astounded at how crowded it was, since it was a week day.

First stop was at the Ranger Station. We'd decided to do a hike recommended by the rangers. They suggested the Nisqually Vista Trail since it was less popular and short. It was early afternoon when we arrived. We could see the haze and smell the smoke from the wildfires in Canada that day. We were told by the rangers that the conditions would not likely improve during the time we were visiting.

The visitor center was at an elevation of 5420 feet. Not necessarily a height where one experiences altitude sickness, but may have contributed to my state of being. Because we had brunch with the family we chose not to stop for lunch. Being borderline hypoglycemic, it is well known that I can become hangry at the drop of a hat. As soon as my sugar level drops I become a stark raving beeeetch. I am usually the last one to notice. I was already aggravated by the people, one of my very favorite things about hiking is to escape the whole social interacting thing. So, when we pulled up and had a hard time finding a parking spot my nervous system took over and much like the Mount Jefferson Caps experience, my mind just screamed $$$@@@&&&###!

Starting on the trail was great! The ranger was correct. There was absolutely no one on the trail. I was immediately relieved. Only a few hundred feet in, I started to feel fatigued. Not just fatigued, but it was as if someone pulled the plug on my energy tank. It was only a quarter mile to the trail loop, with the loop a little over a half mile. The round trip would have been just over a mile.

Feeling like I was walking in a cement body suit drudging through water, it felt like every step labored. We made it to the loop where we were getting shadowed glimpses of Rainier. Mostly the view was just gray, haziness, which resulted in a feeling of suffocation.

Probably another tenth of a mile on the loop I surrendered. I just told Dick I couldn't do it. I know he was disappointed and physically I couldn't really understand what was happening to me. After all, I'd run marathons and he and I regularly hiked 5 to 10 miles at a time with significant elevation gain.

It may have been the first time I listened to my body though and we did a turn around. It was none too soon either with all the factors at play I was a raging b*tch by the time we got back to the car. I may have even let it go too long, but this was the first time that I did a self assessment and situational turn around. I make this a healthy habit these days and have turned around on many hikes since then, especially in the White Mountains. I assess not only for myself but also those I'm hiking with. The point for me is to enjoy the activity and not put myself or those that may have to rescue me or my team members in danger unnecessarily.

After finding food, I was back to myself. Not fun though. I always feel like the Hulk after he's stopped being big and green. Knowing I wasn't myself and had done things I regret, even if I don't remember the details or wasn't really in control at the time.

The place we stayed was amazing. Our own little apartment. Of course, it could be that just because it was clean and private, compared to the In-Tents fiasco, this felt like a five stars experience.

Back to Mount Rainier the next day to hike the Skyline Trail. This is the most popular trail from the Jackson Visitor Center in Paradise. The Loop is 5.5 miles to an elevation of 6800 ft. Most go clockwise so of course we decided to go counterclockwise hoping to not be in the throngs of the crowds. We also got there fairly early so that helped.

We made sure we brought water and food with us so I didn't become Abbizilla again. Not too far into the trail we came across a couple of people who had stopped. As we approached, we could see what caused their halt. A couple of elk. We all just stood in amazement as these gentle giants strolled across the trail. They kept a wary eye on us as they crossed the path we were on and came within feet of us. Immediately, we knew that it was going to be a great day.

The two-legged animals were all abuzz about our encounter and couldn't wait to see what was next. The other couple quickly strode out of sight. We had the whole day and were in no hurry so just took our time taking it all in as we went along. We didn't have to wait too long to come upon some more people at a pause. At first I couldn't see what had their attention.

Then as if they materialized out of nowhere, I saw them. Marmots! I must have taken a dozen pictures of the first one we saw. We talked with a girl and her mother about what the comical little creatures were. Then, wondered how do you pronounce that? As we continued along the trail we'd excitedly point and say "there's another, there's another, there's another, etc…" until we realized that they were all around us.

I found my spirit animal, at least when I'm well fed, and not tired, or around too many people. They were all enjoying just being. Whether lounging on rocks, or in the grass or snacking on the flora. They were not in a rush to go anywhere. They'd get there when they got there. Kind of how I always hike. While Dick was more like a mountain goat, I was much more a marmot. The higher in elevation we went, the more there seemed to be and I delighted at the sight of each and every one we encountered.

We took all the side trips we could. Went up Paradise Glacier Trail up Pebble Creek and back to Panorama Point where we sat a bit and had our lunch. We met a couple of women in ther 80s. They talked about being on a girls day out. They talked about all the fabulous adventures they had been on together. Mostly that they would come up there often. They immediately became my idols. I hope to be like them when I grow up. I think I'm on my way.

They did tell us to come back and how the smoke from Canada was wreaking havoc on the views. They kept apologizing to us as if it was somehow their fault.

I think we had plenty of views even if we didn't get to see all of Rainier in her glory. We did get some views as we were leaving the park. As if the skies opened up just enough to give us a glimpse of what we'd been missing. It was hard to imagine how such a majestic, imposing, and statuesque mass had been there all day, yet not visible to us. It seemed so close when we could see it. We did understand, then, why the women had apologized. For Rainier was magnificent.

THIRD 4000 FOOTER
AND FUN ON THE WATER

Aweek after returning home from the West Coast we were planning a trip back to New Hampshire. Actually, Dick and I were just along for the ride on this one. His friends Linda and Arthur were on a mission to wrap up their 4000 Footers. They had only a few left to go and we got invited to join them for one or two in the upcoming weekend.

It was Arthur and Linda who had introduced Dick to hiking in the White Mountains. Dick had joined them for several of their 4000 Footer accomplishments. Along with another friend of theirs, Sandy, who had joined them on several summit quests. At the time Dick hadn't declared that he was tackling "The List" yet. And I was just blindly following due to peer pressure, kind of.

We were invited to Arthur and Linda's home for a planning dinner a few days before the trip. We went over the plan and Andy added me to his master spreadsheet. There it was, I was officially being tracked and an official 48-4000 Footer peak bagger, whether I liked it or not.

We left Friday afternoon, since Dick was the only one retired at the time. After the four plus hour drive plus stopping for dinner we arrived at a condo that we shared in the Lincoln area. We unloaded our stuff and settled in. We got ready what we could for the next day so that only lunches and water needed to be added to our packs in the morning. Our standard fare for lunch was PBJs. Sandy called dibs on making the sandwiches in the morning.

I had my own pack by then, but Dick carried my water which helped out hugely with my weight. My pack included my lunch, clothes, small first aid kit and my snacks. Snacks included trail mix, granola bar, sunflower seeds, and an apple to round out my lunch. I liked the sunflower seeds because when I was focused on cracking the seeds and separating the nut from the husk, I didn't focus on the fact that I felt like I was dying going up the mountain.

I was not well versed at the time in LNT and yes, would spit my shells out on the trail. Lesson learned and I learned to bring baggy to spit my shells into so that I bring out what I bring in. Later I'd learn the motto, take only pictures, leave only footprints. I'm pretty sure some would like us to not even leave the footprints.

Saturday morning we headed to hike Carrigain. When we got there we found that the access road was closed. This would add an extra four miles to the planned hike. Yes, by now I'm sure you all know what I was yelling in my head. Actually, I'm pretty sure that this time it spilled past my lips.

The first two miles, after the road, was easy and I thought that maybe the extra distance won't be that bad after all. Then, of course, we started going up. The downside of having Dick carry my water was that I had to wait until he was close enough for me to gasp out, "waahhter…"

Of course being unable to breathe while watching my footing and navigating the ascent isn't always an easy thing to do.

The group was most definitely faster afoot than I. Off they'd go with one of them usually staying behind to accompany me. Now to look at me, especially then, one would think that I'd be faster than I am. Being thin and even fit does not equate to being speedy. I'm just a slow and steady sort. Always have been and always will be.

Those that went faster, which is anyone I've ever hiked with, would go ahead, then wait. Of course, by the time I'd catch up they were rested and off they'd go. So, I had to be quick with my gasping request for water which also needed to be audible to secure a bit of hydration.

Coming up the switchbacks I remember Arthur looking particularly concerned about me. I have exercise induced asthma, which I didn't think about at the time. When running I carried a rescue inhaler for those times I'd start wheezing and coughing.

I hadn't considered carrying it with me on a hike until then. It seems like I'm the last one to hear me wheezing. I was just thinking it's normal to become labored going uphill, and that's true, but no one else in the group was wheezing and coughing. Lesson learned, just like when you're running, carry your inhaler.

We reached the open ridge and because there's a peak there, I became excited. I thought we were there. Only to have a boy coming from the other direction say "you're almost there," as he pointed towards the actual summit. Gotta love those false summit experiences. Pretty sure my jaw dropped because it didn't look like we were almost there. Instead it felt like, "it's waaayyy over there."

Now I was no longer wheezing but definitely felt like the wind had been knocked out of me. My excitement had vanished as quickly as a pin popped balloon. Onward we travelled. Before we knew it we were there and the excitement returned, well, until we decided that it wasn't a true summit unless one climbs the fire tower. I have a sad and funny feeling that it was my voice that made that claim.

It was a magnificent view from the top of the tower and well worth the effort.

Coming down the mountain was even tougher than going up. With so much mud and lots of rock hopping there was at least one slip and fall. This may have been when Dick claimed that I had the most spectacular falls.

There was plenty of interesting conversation to keep things moving. Talk about "furries" and discussions about an upcoming wedding where the bride was having a man of honor instead of maid of honor. And many other wonders of the world.

When we got back to the road walk I sat on the side of the wooden bridge with the bottom of my feet on fire. I was sure that there must be open blisters. Thankfully there were not any open wounds and another lesson learned.

Stick to the footwear you know. I had new boots, which I had worn before but not on a big mountain hike, they weren't for me. I'd had Merrell waterproof moabs before and decided to try the non-waterproof ones. The non-waterproof fit just enough differently that my feet slid in my boots and caused the bottom of my feet to blister. They became a very expensive equipment fail and new gardening footwear.

We managed the two miles back to the car and enjoyed a well deserved meal at one of the local breweries. It was in the next couple of days that I realized that part of my difficult descent was attributed to being infected with Lyme Disease once again. That was probably my sixth time having active Lyme. One of the hazards of being an outdoors person in New England.

We were originally supposed to do Mount Madison but opted for Plan B. After a bit more distance than planned, we were all sufficiently beat up that we agreed we weren't up for tackling another mountain. We decided to spend the day playing on the Saco River.

It paid to be flexible. We all had a grand time and I highly recommend it. Dick and I shared a double kayak. We didn't do too badly together. No one ended up in the water that didn't want to be in the water.

What do you do with four engineers in the evening? Put puzzles together of course. At least that's what we did. I'd say it was a nice end to a perfect weekend. We stayed up until it was done. Very satisfying, just not necessarily relaxing. And those of us not retired had to return to working for a living.

SEPTEMBER SUMMITS
IN THE WHITES

A few weeks later Dick and I returned to New Hampshire. We now had a place to stay since Dick had bought a condo in Lincoln. We took it somewhat easy and tackled Tecumseh. Ah, the proverbial staircase not quite to heaven but close. I do appreciate the hard work it took to put steps in just for us summit seekers. A fine staircase indeed though there was no real break just a constant up as you go. It was kind of a miracle that there was no asthma attack, just a tough and steady out of breathness kind of day.

It had rained early before we got on the trail. The trail stayed wet all day. We had a lunchtime guest at the summit. It was the cutest little red squirrel we ever did see, Even though I'm partial to redheads, we didn't share our eats, much to the little fellow's disappointment.

It was definitely slippery on the way down. We decided to go down the aptly named Waterville Valley ski slope. There were quite a few slip-n-slide moments. We also had some great views so the day was not a loss. As we plodded down "The Boneyard" to "The Lower

Periphery," we were gifted some scenic outlooks. The views helped make up for the soggy conditions.

My count was up to 4 out of 48. Perhaps I was on my way after all.

Arthur and Linda came up the next day and we took a trip to Artists Bluff, not a 4000 Footer but a highly recommended hike. As we looked out we could easily see how it got its name. Wishing I had an easel and knew how to make good use of it. This was intended as a little warm up hike because the next day was Arthur and Linda's grand finale. As luck would have it as I was cruising down from the bluff I landed on the side of my foot and twisted my ankle, knee, achilles, you name it, all kinds of snap, crackles, and pops. I went down hard.

After hobbling the rest of the way out and making it to the car we headed to Littleton. The plan was to eat at the Schilling Beer Co. At least, I was going to eat there, the others would also indulge in libations. It was a little too early for dinner when we arrived so we went down to the Ammonoosuc River. The cool water was just what the doctor ordered. I found the perfect spot to sit and soak the injured limb. I'm pretty sure there was some pixie dust in the river that day. I was convinced that I'd have to sit out the next day and stay in the condo with Sport. I sat an hour or so in the magic river and was able to walk out like nothing had happened. The next morning I was good to go.

We had pretty much perfected our night before and morning of preparedness ritual by then. The only thing to do in the morning was make the PBJs, fill the water contairs, and pack up the cooler for the after hike parking lot celebration. In the morning it was my turn to make the PBJs. We all took turns filling our bladders with ice, then topped off with water. Arthur was in charge of the cooler. After each hike, when we returned to the car, we would have a little tailgate party. Besides drinks, we'd enjoy some cookies, either made by Linda, or open a bag of Tates. Arthur always made sure there was a non-alcoholic something for me. Dick wasn't always so thoughtful, probably an early sign of how things might turn out.

Middle Carter was Arthur and Linda's FINAL 4000 Footer to complete the NH 48. It was a little cool to start, as it should be in early autumn. It was also moist but not really rainy. Just humid enough all day for everything to stay wet.

We went up Northern Imp to the Imp Cliff and that felt pretty easy. The first mile was relatively flat and on the second mile, even with an 800ft plus elevation gain, we remained steady even with the trail a bit rocky and rooty. From North Imp we went to Imp Face and then onto North Carter Trail and finally followed the Carter-Moriah Trail to Middle Carter.

Dick and I had gone to the Woodstock Inn a couple days earlier where one of their specialized drinks was 4000 Footer Beer. Dick brought the beer for Arthur and Linda to enjoy at the top. Then gave them a couple pint glasses when we got to the bottom. It was a nice gesture and taught me how to celebrate someone's finish with what suits them.

There are really no views from the summit of Middle Carter and I venture that most people usually make a day of a Carter traverse. I'm actually wondering if Arthur and Linda are the only people to have ever finished an out and back on Middle Carter?

We made sure to get pictures of the finishers next to the under-whelming cairn that let us know we were at the summit. Yes, we did miss it at first. The happy couple shared their summit beverage. They usually share anyways, but one doesn't want to be tipsy navigating down any mountain.

It didn't seem as bad going up as it did coming down. Perhaps because I was tired but on the way down everything caused me to slip. Even without being impaired I had a hard enough time staying on my feet on the descent. As a matter of fact, not too far from the summit, I pulled one of my spectacular falls. No one saw it but they all heard the laughter. I ended up in a bed of bushy shrubbery. As if it'd been waiting to catch me. Probably the softest landing I've had to date.

We did have a bite to eat at the summit but didn't linger because of lack of views from the top. We decided to find a more inviting place to celebrate when we got to the bottom. After all, it is only once you've gone up and down on your own power can you consider a peak officially bagged anyway. There was a picnic table conveniently located at the bottom near the parking lot. We enjoyed a summit or rather after summit lunch in this case in comfort. Arthur and Linda enjoyed their surprise and I felt honored to be part of their journey.

I offered to make the PBJs for our next hike but was informed that I use too much peanut butter. I still don't understand having too much peanut butter in a PBJ, it's like saying there is too much cheese on a pizza. Unintentionally, of course, I was off PBJ duty from then on.

We had a day's rest after Middle Carter and it was back to just Dick and I. I decided to take a few days off work and keep playing in the mountains. We had hoped to add the Kinsman(s) to the done list. Not sure what time we started. We pulled into the parking area and it was full, so we had to drive down and find parking on the other side of Route 3.

We started up the Lonesome Lake Trail. It was another cool day and I started with lots of layers that came off quickly and I was dragging butt even with the day's rest. There were several other hikers on the trail. We played leap frog with a few others but not too long in we caught up to a group of boys and a few adults with them. I knew before we got close that they were boy scouts, having been a den mother with Peter's troop and attending many group events. They would rush ahead, then STOP, just STOP right there in the middle of the trail.

So, we hung back the first time or two that we saw them do this. Then we were right behind them so decided to just try and go thru and hopefully just continue. We were ahead of them for a short while when they just barreled past us only to STOP once more. There were a couple of young women that we ended up chatting with who were in the same predicament as us and kind of lagged behind the troop.

After a couple of these very annoying stop and waits Dick went up to the troop leader, or at least one of the adults to ask if they planned to do this all the way up the trail. The answer was "we can only go as fast as our slowest member. "

And the woman stated "You can go ahead of us." To which I replied. "We already tried that."

I suppose it was just the spark they needed. For once they started again we didn't see them for the next half mile or so. By the time we saw then again we had arrived at the junction to Lonesome Lake. We left them at the crossroads and went to the Lonesome Lake Hut with the two young women. The women decided to go on to the Kinsmans. After checking the weather, we decided that the better course of action for us was to head to Cannon Mountain. I felt bad that Dick wouldn't get another 4000 Footer under his belt because he'd already done Cannon. I was grateful for the decision because it felt more doable than trying to tackle two mountains that day.

From the Lonesome Lake Trail we took Kinsman Ridge Trail up to Cannon. Along the way we crossed paths with a couple of guys with their kids. One had a daughter and one a son. They (the kids that is) were young. I'd guess 8 or so and they took it all in stride. Much better than I fared. Each rocky scramble chipped away at what remaining energy I had. The tank was reading empty and I made it to the summit without anything in reserve.

There was a lodge with bar and restaurant and hordes of folks that took the tram to the summit. It was a bit frustrating trying to get a photo on the platform at the summit after being spent and then trying to get a free spot without "those" people in it. But we prevailed, got my photo up on the platform and headed in. I got a hot chocolate and Dick got a beer to go with our PBJs. We saw the gentlemen with the kids and I overheard the men talking about taking the tram down. That sounded good to me, but then I knew I'd have to do it all over again and my energy level was coming back thanks to the comforts of the lodge.

We headed down on the Hi-Cannon Trail. There were some tricky spots, like where the wooden ladder resided. I still believe it was a better trail to come down on. Fewer Giant Rock scrambles to descend.

There was something very poetic in seeing the kids at their campfire in the campgrounds on our way to the car. What were the chances of seeing them again? There they were toasting marshmallows as we gave them a nod as we strode past. I wonder what stories they will tell of that day? Hotdogs at the summit, the tram ride down, eating apples on the rocks on the way up, or just simply spending time with their dads?

TAKING A BREAK
FROM WINTER WEATHER

While fall gave way to Winter, Dick and I decided to escape where it was warm for a bit. We settled on Costa Rica and I found a travel package that would provide us with a taste of excitement and everything exploratory they had to offer. I decided to book the Adventure Tour through Costa Rican Trails. They managed everything and all we needed to do was book our own flights and show up at the transfer locations on time. As always, the first adventure was getting there.

Our first day was a LOOOONG one. Up at 4:00 am, 45-minute drive to the airport. The original flight was delayed so we missed our connection to Charlotte by just minutes. There was only one flight from Charlotte to San Jose so we were in a bit of a panic. What was so disconcerting was the manner in which we were dismissed. The woman at the gate pointed at the plane as it was pulling away from the ramp and said that she did try to get them to wait but then told us we had to go to the kiosk to find a new flight. So, off the kiosk only to have it state that we needed to find an agent. Wouldn't you know that the agent that sent us to the kiosk disappeared like a well planned Houdini trick.

After waiting in line for an hour with all the other people from our delayed flight, we were re-routed through Miami so we could make it to Costa Rica the day we were supposed to. Guess that was technically the following day back home. Otherwise, we would have had to get in a day late and not sure what could have been done with our itinerary. Everything was managed through the travel agency including our transportation and accommodations once we arrived in Costa Rica.

We made it into the San Jose airport by the skin of our teeth. After we missed our connecting flight and as soon as I had our new flights scheduled, I called the Cost Rican Trails office. We thought we'd see someone with a sign with our names at the baggage pickup area in San Jose. We did pass a woman with names on a sign so Dick suggested asking her. She directed us to the tourism desk and she called the travel agent to make sure all was good. She said someone would be outside waiting for us. Dick was skeptical, because once you leave the baggage area and go outside, you're not allowed back inside. Sure enough, we passed through customs and there was someone waiting to take us to the Park Inn Hotel. Whew, relief washed over us and we couldn't wait to see how the rest of the trip was going to go.

INTO THE RAIN FOREST

Late to bed and early to rise. We were up by 5:00 the next morning. Costa Rica's time zone was one hour later, so at least that's something (I always get that messed up, it would have been 6:00 am back home.) The wakeup call was a half hour earlier than we asked which was okay by me since I like being early anyway. It also gave us time for breakfast. Pepe from Pacuare Lodge met us in the lobby. There was one other couple there and then we stopped to pick up another group of four. We drove for an hour and a half through beautiful areas where the lifestyle looked like a great way to live. There were gardens all along the hillsides, built into mountain sides with a lot of houses built out of simple materials. It made me think of the LA area where there were switchback roads and the houses were almost built right into the hillsides. Lots of bananas, and sugarcane. I loved seeing the terraces for planting. It was how I imagined the Mayans and Aztecs must have lived. Beautiful and functioning.

We stopped for breakfast where we had the "typical" Costa Rican meal. Beans and rice with scrambling eggs, cheese (I think it was cheese), coffee for me and black tea for Dick. The meal was complete with the most delicious fresh fruit. After we were back on the road we stopped and saw a sloth up in a tree. Pepe was a story teller and jokester. We all got out of the van to have a look at the sloth and Pepe called it his employee and said that it needed to get to work.

The van took us to the river and from there we had to divide up into rafts to get to Pacuare Lodge. While we were waiting for the rest of the group Dick and I did a bit of walking around some rocks near the river and headed over to the little pool where Michael and Ashley were hanging out. They were a nice young couple on their honeymoon. Originally we were set to raft with them, since there was an older group of four that had joined us on shuttle. But the group we were waiting for was a family of 14, well 13 of them were rafting with the group. Ashley and Michael joined the four that were on our shuttle while Dick and I were the odd ones out. Soooo… we ended up with a family of four who were part of the big group. A mom, dad and two girls I'm guessing around 11 & 13 or so. Oh my goodness, the Dad was just clueless. Originally, I sat behind the dad, Dick dubbed him a "dork" and when we recounted the events. One would have thought it was the girls that didn't listen, but not in this case. Our raft guide was Ricardo. He was so great. And such patience. The commands he tried to teach us were, "Forward, Backward, Left side back, (the right side needs to paddle forward during those times) and Right side back, (you guessed it, left side paddle forward)."

When we first got in the rafts we were told to sit on the side and secure our feet in the supports on the floor of the boat. The dorky Dad (DD) kept sliding onto the support, where my foot was underneath. Three times in a row, I tapped him on his side and got him back up on the side of the raft. Plus, he was not paying attention to Ricardo. Ricardo would call out a command we'd pretty much be done before DD got his paddle in the water. The fourth time DD sat on the support and essentially my foot I yell "I can't sit here" and made Dick switch with me. Thank goodness Dick was a good sport and way more patient than I.

The youngest girl was great and kept telling of how there were 14 of them on the trip together. Mostly from Canada. She told us about everything they'd already seen. All four types of monkeys in Costa Rica, howlers, spider, squirrel, and white face. She even jumped into the water when Ricardo said it was OK. Of course Mom panicked a little, but Mom did a good job pulling her back into the raft. Her older sister however let us all know how she didn't like "spinning" or "going backwards" after Ricardo got us spinning (once on purpose). She didn't seem to understand that this was not a ride at Disney. That the river takes us where it wants and that we needed to just go along with it.

After five miles on the river we arrived at Pacuare Lodge. An ecofriendly Lodge on the National Geographic 25 List. We didn't really know how it was going to work, if activities were included or not. I remember seeing a first itinerary that said they were. We were told we could pick one afternoon activity that started at 2:30pm. Lunch was served at 1pm. We arrived at the lodge right around noon. Thankfully Ricardo grabbed our bags because we wanted to tip him anyways for the masterful way he dealt with DD, anxious Mom, and self-righteous girl. We had the greatest little bungalow overlooking the river. Perfect setup with a hammock in the entrance with a sign welcoming us with our names on it.

The food was all so magnificent. Everything fresh and prepared five-star restaurant style. They knew who we were by name, so sat down and brought what we'd ordered on the drive to the rafts. We chose to do the hike to the waterfalls for our first activity. Luckily we got to join Ashley and Michael and another young couple who mostly spoke German along the way. Our guide was probably the ONLY one that we found "non-enthusiastic." He was pretty deadpan. When Dick asked about all the other activities and what other things he did he only answered "I'm a naturalist. I don't do any other activities." We were relieved by this answer.

After much consternation we decided our First activity the next day would be a hike up to the indigenous village. We knew we wanted to hike and had contemplated going to the hidden waterfalls. After our deadpan guide gave us the crazy sign when he talked about it we chose the next longest hike. We later found out that only a few guests have ever made it as far as the falls, so we knew we'd made the right choice. The Carveci tribe had quite a few members employed by the Pacuare Lodge and we were lucky to get one of the members as our guide. Ashley and Michael opted for the hike into the Costa Rican (not native's) village.

I don't mind reiterating that the meals were all magnificent. I tried to stick to selections that were as authentic as possible, understanding that they were catered to the tourists. For dinner we ate by the bonfire. We had a great position where you could feel the heat from the fire. We enjoyed it for a while until it started to rain causing us to move underneath a tree.

In the morning we had a "typical" breakfast with fruit and caffe con leche. Met up with Giovanni (Greg) and William (Win or Juan) as our guides. Win was from the village that we were going to visit. As we hiked up to the Carveci Village we got to see leaf cutter ants, a garter snake, giant dragon flies, bullet ants and mahogany trees. It was good to see and hear about all the conservation efforts as well as the huge effort from the Pacuare Lodge's owner on working with the locals. The Pacuare Lodge employs many indigenous people and people from the nearby towns. We saw Win's house from a distance. Pacuare Lodge not only employs many but helps develop work with the community.

We brought some sandwiches up as "snacks" and left a couple with the Carvecians. We got to see some plants that they used for medicine and see how they used plants for building material. They used palm leaves to cover the roofs. The leaves often do a better job keeping the water out than many synthetic materials do. After the leaves are laid on the roof, there's a fire built in the center of the structure. This helps get the insects out of the roof and causes the leaves to stick together to reinforce the waterproofing. Gourds are hollowed out and used for containers and decorations. There are gardens built on the trees themselves by securing moss. We saw some of the most beautiful orchids growing this way. There are trees all around that have beautiful orange-red blossoms that were currently in bloom. I can't remember the native name but in English are called "fire trees."

We did see a sloth in the distance on our hike the first day. We were spoiled by seeing one on the drive to the rafts thinking that they'd be everywhere. We were hoping to see more when we played in the canopy. Yes, we ziplined up amongst the treetops and had a chance to fly through the rainforest.

FROM VOLCANOS TO
BLACK SAND BEACHES

After breakfast we loaded back on the rafts for our departure. Next stop was at the volcano Arenal. Our resort in LaFortuna gave us a front row seat to this formerly very active volcano. The resort was very romantic with the towels folded into swans staged on the bed to greet us when we entered. The picture window framed Arenal perfectly and I could only imagine laying in bed and watching the fiery smokey show. It was still a beautiful sight to see, even if there was no volcanic activity.

A tropical paradise awaited us at the café where we watched exotic birds come and feed while we ourselves dined. In the morning there were peacocks, parrots, and other fowl that I didn't know their names already awaiting their breakfast. They were demanding it actually. We found a table to enjoy their spectacle while getting fueled for our day. Afterwards, we lounged by the pool and watched an iguana take a slow stroll through the gardens.

We took a guided hike around Arenal. They brought us up as high as the safety zone. Our guide talked about the original eruption in 1968 and how two small villages had been buried. He told us about boulders as big as houses that had landed up to a half mile away from the initial eruption. Arenal continued to be active until 2010, it was January of 2019 at the time, so we only missed any activity by nine years. To which he added, "you never know when she might wake up again."

Our hike on and around the volcano brought us to a pineapple grove. We learned how the farmers will place bags over the plants to facilitate blooming and fruit production. What a sweet way to end the tour.

In the evening we headed to the hot water springs. The springs were heated by the magma still close enough to the surface to tap into it's thermal reserves. It was a perfect place to relax. There were so many pools and I think we tried each and every one.

We took a long van ride to our coastal experience. This landed us on a black sand beach. Which was beautiful but as you can imagine, hot underfoot. We walked down the beach to see what was in the surrounding area. This brought us to a little gem of a store that was just a bit more than a shack, ironically named, The Shack. Then down on the roadway that ran parallel to the beach we found a brewery for Dick and some local eateries for me.

That evening I had the following thoughts. As I sit overlooking the Pacific, listening to the birds and the waves, watching the sunset with all the colors that pop thru. Noticing how there's a red hue in the transition between the sand and the surf. Watching dogs who seem to have no owners and are allowed to roam, seeming to have no particular place to go or anyone to call their own, but just are. I think that this is how Hemingway must have been inspired. To sit along a seaside beach and observe, of course, he also had a little help from liquid libations. I came to understand how he could let his imagination go!

As the sunlight was fading, it became harder to see my paper but the silhouettes became clearer. And because people don't behave, I had what would have been a perfect picture of a family's silhouette with the Pacific and twilight as the background.

Even as I was surrounded by beautiful sights and sounds I focused on my little inconveniences. Like where I smashed my toe into the steps at the hot water springs, and all the little bug bites that annoy me to no end. Resulting in not focusing on watching the dragon flies or the pelicans. Then, I pushed all of my annoyances away and focused once more on the pelicans as they would soar, find a fish, dive then just float on the water. I swear I could almost hear them go "ahhh…"

Then came the skidoos… People ruin everything. I was annoyed once more.

Next, we were scheduled to take a cruise and do some cool water activities. It turned out to be mostly just a booze cruise. There was a bright spot to the day, when we reached the lagoon and were allowed to go into the water. Dick and I opted for a bit of snorkeling. Others played on watercraft, kayaks and paddleboards. Though it didn't last as long as I would have liked.

Being afraid of the water, it takes me time to ease in and get comfortable, even with a life jacket. I never let the fear stop me, but it does take time to work through. So of course by the time I was able to enjoy paddling around and finding a little school of fish to observe, we were being told to get back on the boat. Dick's response was to hop aboard a paddleboard and do laps around the boat. Which many found a hoot as I acted like a mother to an errant child. I finally conceded to the fact that we were there for a good time, and he was quite entertaining, so I joined in with those that enjoyed his antics.

Our final breakfast at the shore we had overlooking the beach. Following with some time to relax and enjoy our Morning of Leisure according to our itinerary.

A bit of an observation as we lazed upon the shore. I call it *A Tale of Tails*. Hope you enjoy!

There was a woman whom I dubbed Madame Hartlett with her canine. The pooch was an adorable springer spaniel who we shall call Drea. After spreading out her blanket, The Hartlett trotted to the water with Drea at her heels. Madame plunged into the sea while Drea hesitated. Drea followed her in up to where the surf turned foamy, from there held his ground and barked incessantly at her. Pretty sure Drea was saying "what the @#$% are you doing out there? Get back here where it's safe."

Drea reluctantly gives up and makes his way back to the blanket. He takes to the blanket and makes himself comfortable. When Madame finally comes back up it's just to disrupt Drea. She proceeds to shoo him off the blanket, just to head right back to the water.

Meanwhile, two of the three amigos, Anton and Pedro came traipsing up the sandy highway. The three amigos were free spirited scamps who were often scrounging in the area. They were in fact, up in the resort area that very morning, looking to score a free breakfast. Now that Anton and Pedro were back in the area, they decided to park themselves near the blanket. Anton and Pedro are content just sitting, perhaps they pick that spot figuring that if there's already a dog there then the humans will share something with them. This rational seemed to work, since soon enough, some of the other vacationers stroll over to pet the amigos.

The Hartlett proceeds to drag Drea into the water. She finally lets him go and Drea scurries back to the blanket. Anton and Pedro look at each other as if to say, "ah, this is why we leave our humans at home."

The third amigo, Artemis, arrives. They hang for a while and it's clear to see that even though Artemis is the smallest of the crew, he's indeed the ring leader. Artemis gives the signal and they head up the beach.

A few moments later a black and white dog comes along and distracts Drea. The three amigos circle back around and pass back by following a group of people. The black and white dog brings Drea along and they go to meet up with the pack. Madame Hartlett was not very happy, but I found it rather amusing. Farewell fine pups.

MUSINGS AND FAREWELL TO COSTA RICA

It was time to return to our day to day life. On the long trip home I dared to venture into reflection.

It's easy to glamorize Costa Rica with its warm temperatures, tropical flora and fauna. Every landscape possessed its own charm whether rain forest, mountains, beaches, or fields stretching as far as the eye can see. Many of the structures are simple, either concrete, wooden (with the feel that they could have been constructed of pallets taken apart and reconstructed to make walls) or just ridged metal. Almost all roofs were of metal, some rusted to give the look and feel as if they've withstood the test of time. It's the colors that are the most amazing as if somehow they are richer than anywhere else in the world.

As a matter of fact, everything is alive with color. Yellows, reds, blues, white, and even the browns seem to be more pronounced than anywhere else that I've been. Is it because the green of the trees and the plants don't want to be overshadowed that the other colors beg for you to see them? Or are the people here themselves more colorful, so why not show on the outside what they have inside?

So many people were in San Jose, which you forget about the city after being in paradise. Still there was lots of greenery and growing things to be seen. The mountains not only line the city, but merge with it. Still colorful in the city. There are iron fences (or barriers as our former fearful leader would call them) around every structure though. Not sure if it's because of homelessness, crime, or pest control? Like Dick says it doesn't give you a feeling that you're safe to walk around.

Some things that I've learned
- Don't throw toilet paper in the toilet
  - Some places say because it will clog
  - Others say because they are practicing environmental control
- Living posts
  - There's a plant they can cut to posts and will grow
  - Provides shade for animals
- Leaf cutter ants are amazing
  - Big ants carry little ants on the leaves
  - They don't eat the leaves but secrete something to attract other bugs for food
  - Dick just read that little ants are not for quality control like he thought but for protection from flies that will lay eggs on heads and larvae will feed on ants
- Bullet ants are the biggest and baddest bugs that we ran into
  - Don't let them bite
  - Kinda made me feel bad for sending Dick really close to get a picture
- There weren't any mosquitos, at least as far as we could tell

- Arenal was active from 1968-2010 with eruptions of red lava. Conflicting how many volcanoes are active and what does "being active" mean
- Toucans are NOT NICE
  - Costa Rican people don't care for them because they push birds out of their nests and eat the eggs
  - Though they are a favorite of tourists
- Things don't dry in the rain forest
- Day of Leisure translates to A LONG DAY of travel
- Rubber boots are a must when hiking in the rainforest

In the airport, besides overpriced souvenirs they still have pay phones. It was kind of sad to see at the Pacuare Lodge that technology has invaded the jungle. Though it's just in one area, you can see folks (the guides especially) pull out their phones and are lost to the big sucking sound of their handheld devices. I was glad we didn't have a TV at least.

When we made it onto the flight and the mood to write was finally upon me, it was too bumpy and too dark. And the ass in front of me decided he needed to put the seat back. That ass of course was Dick. Then it became too dark to continue and I couldn't reach my light. Goodnight and goodbye dear Costa Rica. Perhaps we'll meet again.

BACK TO THE
WHITE MOUNTAINS

Our adventures abroad were fabulous, but it is the White Mountain range that takes hold of my sense of wonderment. In March of 2019 we decided to start working on the 52 with a view (52WAV) list. I initially ran across this list when doing online research about the 4000 Footer list. It was on this trip that I first met The Mountain Wanderer. On our way to Dick's condo, we decided to stop into the Mountain Wanderer Book & Maps store. It was my great honor and pleasure to meet Steve Smith, the owner of the bookstore, author of the White Mountain Guide, and official Mountain Wanderer. I now never miss an opportunity to visit whenever I'm in or passing through Lincoln. I always check to see if the flag is out showing that The Mountain Wanderer is open for business.

Back to March of 2019, I decided to pick up my own White Mountain Trail Map by Map Adventures and loved laying it out to help find new places to explore. Dick and I often collaborated on potential outings and would come up with several options to choose from. I also picked up my own copy of The White Mountain Guide. I really got into checking the trail info, distance, estimated time, description of the terrain. We started comparing how long it would take us versus how long the time was estimated in the book. That was always a fun game.

We decided to journey up Hedgehog Mountain as our first officially planned 52WAV hike. It was our first experience hiking a mountain with snow in the Whites. Dick had told me about the monorails but experiencing them was a whole different ballgame. Sandy had come up and decided to join us on our First 52WAV journey up Hedgehog Mountain. Well, we found out the hard way what it was all about.

The good old White Mountain monorail. Not to be confused with the Walt Disney World monorail. While the later is a fun way to travel, traveling on the monorail in The White Mountains is a trip all on its own. The monorail in the Whites is created by compacting the snow on the trails that build after every snowfall throughout the winter.

I've come to believe that the life of a monorail in the Whites has three phases.

1. Developmental – This is the forming stage and happens all winter as the snow falls over and over again. Those who are hearty and enjoy breaking trail will head out with their trusty snowshoes to stomp out the trail. As this happens time and time again, the trail can end up being several feet deep.

2. Established – The glory days usually begin within a couple of days after a significant snowfall on a well-travelled trail. The hard packed track may become firm and smooth enough to no longer need snowshoes. Though that doesn't stop me from wearing mine. There are snow bridges formed and all roots, rocks, and waterways become forgotten.

3. Fading – The end of life for these footpath highways is wrought with strife. The once mighty passageway gives way to sinking cavities, collapsing bridges, and narrowing paths. A good spruce trap thrown in on occasion just to keep things interesting. Then, as things begin to warm and the snow begins to melt, the monorail is the last man standing. Remnants may last well into spring and occasionally into early summer. Then we wonder if they were real or just imagined.

4. wtf

Yes, I know I said three, and it really is three. Shoulder season has its own rules and is what they typically call spring because you're in transition out of winter, but not necessarily free of winter conditions. Therefore, any and every season could, would, and will be experienced. Coincidentally, we'd just embarked on shoulder season so were in a constant phase four.

As we headed up the trail on our attempt to summit Hedgehog Mountain our trail started in phase two and we were fine as long as we didn't stray off the trail. The monorail at the time was the same level as the remaining snow and you only realized you weren't on it when a step landed you thigh high off the side. This is affectionately referred to as post holing. Because, as the name suggests you leave behind what looks like a hole worthy of setting a fence post. The severity of said post hole is completely dependent on the depth and condition of the snow. If the monorail is well established then you can almost easily tell when you've stepped off and creating post holes is not necessarily voluntary. However, with new snowfall some choose to posthole their way up the mountains instead of using snowshoes right after a fresh snowfall, then one does not contribute to creating the monorail, but instead creates postholes, that could freeze and become ice-holes. Therefore, I implore folks to not be an ice-hole

The deeper and softer the snow, it only follows to reason, the deeper the post hole. This is also one of the greatly debated topics in the White Mountain hiking community. I was content to be oblivious to the chatter at the time. I now have very strong opinions on winter habits on the trail, which will be discussed ad nauseum in the following chapters.

On the trip up we stayed mostly on top of the well-established monorail. We were granted amazing views from East Ledges, the summit and Allen's Ledge. The weather was perfect, which led to a bit of softening of the snow. On the way down there was an area where Dick and Judy had gotten ahead of me, this was par for the course. I was still on the monorail when I took a step forward and sunk up to my waist. It did take the both of them to help pull me back out of the hole. There were a couple of thigh higher post holes before the mother holer!

Dick had heard about black fly season and that it typically started after the snow melts. Therefore, we decided to wait until after June to hit the trails again. By mid-July we were itching to get back to it. On our return we stopped in at the Mountain Wanderer. Dick asked about black fly season and whether Steve thought it was over. Steve's response was that they seemed to have skipped black fly season and gone right into mosquito season and said it was the worst he'd ever seen.

The whole crew came up, Arthur, Linda, and Sandy and we were able to get some nice hikes in with Sport joining the fun. After a day of rain we hiked up to Franconia Falls along the Pemigewasset River. This was a pleasant hike in Lincoln Woods. Yes, I did enjoy this easy level section of wooded open path area the first few times I encountered it.

The day was warm and wet, but that's why we chose this hike. Weather called for rain so we didn't want to be in any open areas or worry about slick rocks and roots while trying to go up and down anything challenging.

The next day it was going to be hot so we wanted something that Sport could do and would have some water to cool off in. We picked another couple 52WAVs, Jennings Peak and Sandwich Mountain. It was decided on Drake Brooks Trail for the way up. Plenty of water for Sport. When we reached the intersection with Sandwich Mountain Trail, we had 0.2 mi to Jennings Peak. Hence, the rest of the trip became "only 0.2 mi" whenever we wanted to know "How much farther?"

There were beautiful views from both Jennings Peak and Sandwich Dome. Returned by way of Sandwich Mountain Trail.

Another day, another 52WAV. Three days of hiking and three more 52WAVs.

I was due to have surgery a couple weeks later so it was nice to get some good hiking in before I was to be out of commission.

PRE-PANDEMIC OUTINGS

Only after trying noninvasive methods, I was finally scheduled for surgery to fix a long occurring health issue. The surgery was planned for Thursday, August 1st. The company I worked for, of course, made getting an approved leave of absence as difficult as possible. After proving to this outside company that the surgery and recovery time was necessary, they still hadn't given their approval. I continued to call daily and finally spoke to someone Friday before my surgery and got the old "you need to provide this one last form…"

Monday morning, just a few days before the surgery, I went to the post office to mail out this last form needed. As I was driving through the last intersection before getting to work, BAM, someone runs the red light and T-bones me. Just like that, car was totaled, luckily I wouldn't need a vehicle for a while I was recouping anyways. So, I got to have a tour of the hospital before going in as planned. Luckily, nothing serious from the accident, I was just a bit banged up.

Back to the hospital I went, for the scheduled event this time. Surgery was a success. Waking up almost wasn't. The anesthesia did not want to let me go and I didn't wake up from my 6:00 am surgery until around 2:30 pm. Then the opioids kicked my butt. No chance this gal will abuse those. Couldn't even keep them in my system, couldn't keep ANYTHING in my system. A longer stay in the hospital than I was hoping for but found out some valuable information about myself. My nurse was an angel and helped figure out that the opioids was causing me a problem.

After a few weeks of bedrest at home, headed up to New Hampshire for some convalescing. We were there about a week when Dick figured he'd hike up to Carter Dome and South Carter with a trip to Mount Hight on a lollypop loop. I was feeling pretty good so decided to join him for part of the hike. I was able to go up the Nineteen Mile Brook Trail without issue. We made it to the junction where Dick went left and onto his summits. I was feeling much better than I thought I would. There hadn't been anything technical or challenging up to the junction, well other than the UP. I decided to keep going towards the Carter Notch Hut. I told myself that I'd turn around whenever I needed or wanted to. It was pretty rock scrambly from the junction to the hut and I just took it one boulder at a time. Had my lunch and contemplated waiting for Dick, since I knew he'd be passing through that way. Knowing I was going much slower than when I started and didn't want to feel like I was holding him back on the descent, I headed back down. Which turned out to be the right decision. I had only made it back to the car and opened the door as Dick immerged from the woods. Yes, we virtually finished at the same time. In conclusion, I did make it to the hut, but it was foolish and a bit reckless.

I was reminded of my Dad's stubbornness streak many years before that. How, after a major heart attack he was allowed out of the hospital and in the family's charge if we promised to keep him from climbing any stairs and that he not be under any stress. My wedding was in a couple of days, and he would be allowed to walk me down the aisle. We assured the doctor that we'd make sure he didn't overdo his activity level.

The morning after we'd brought him home, we went to get him for breakfast. He wasn't in the room we'd made for him on the first floor. We were all in a bit of a panic. Everyone scattered to the winds to find him. I would check in the house with my Mom. While the rest of the family went outside and checked around the house, out in the apple orchard, down at the pond, and along the fields out back.

Then I heard a yell from outside "what are you doing up there?"

He'd gone upstairs, out his bedroom window and climbed onto the porch roof.

I bolted upstairs and met him at the window. After giving him a proper scolding asked, "what the hell were you thinking?"

His answer was, "I just wanted to see if I could."

So, there I was, having climbed up into the mountains just to see if I could. Yes, I am my father's daughter. Then, I understood the sense of accomplishment he'd felt and was proud to follow in his footsteps, so to speak.

It was only after being scolded by my primary doctor did I understand that things could have gone very much awry. She explained that I had only stitches holding my insides together and that the "healing" wouldn't be done for a few more weeks after that.

Only a week after the Carter Notch Hut foolishness, Dick, I and Sport successfully hiked North and South Doublehead from the 52WAV list. Though I felt good about the endeavor, I was probably still pushing the envelope.

Twelve weeks after the surgery I was given the all clear from my doctor, with a clear conscience and healing body, decided to head back up and hit a couple 4000 Footers before going back to work full time. During that trip we stopped at The Mountain Wanderer and picked up the newly published 52WAV book. We enjoyed reading about the trail descriptions the same way we enjoyed reading trail descriptions in The 4000 Footer Guidebook. As a matter of fact, we had purchased The 4000 Footer Guidebook at the time because up till then we'd just borrow Arthur and Linda's book. After visiting with Steve we headed over to Lahout's Summit Shop and thanks to the advice and help of Chuck, I bought my first set of microspikes.

We had selected the North and South Hancocks for our next adventure. Jill, who coordinated the Outdoor Doggo Hikes in Connecticut, had come up and was going to accompany us. Sport and Jill's dog Banjo joined in the fun. The completion would make our 4000 Footer tally as follows: #7 & 8 for me; #40 & 41 for Dick; #9 & 10 for Jill.

The total hike ended up taking almost nine hours. The first couple of miles was a nice walk in the woods. I took out my phone to take a picture at a place that captured my view of Dick and Jill and the pups as they disappeared into a magical and mystical section of the trail. I know that location was somewhere after mile two because my Map my Run App had recently said that we'd finished the second mile in 40 min. Sometime after mile three I started thinking that I should be hearing our three mile pace from my phone at any time. But I didn't want to check just thinking that maybe we were going slower than expected. So, at three and a half miles, when we came to the trail marker I went to pull out my phone. That was when I noticed my pouch was open and the phone was gone.

Dick and Jill asked if I wanted to retrace our steps and go back to search for it. Knowing we'd pass back through that way I said that we could just keep an eye open when we returned. I knew it would take all my strength to get up and back. My hopes were that we'd find it, but at the end of the day it was just a thing and could be replaced. Though it will be a pain in the ass to reload all my quick access stuff.

Onward and upward. Pretty uneventful to the North Peak, just a clamber over/under some downed trees. There were folks at the summit already and we stayed back to enjoy our summit snacks while they went ahead. Then the walk to the South Peak had LOTS of blowdowns. Kind of like an obstacle course. Made it an interesting and fun trek.

On the South Peak we caught up to the same people from North Peak. They were on their way out when we arrived. A bunch of young people came in and took over. They were enjoying their summit snacks and we thought they'd head right out. Instead, they started taking their clothes off. And mind you it was cold, with a capital K. It had snowed on the peaks the night before. Apparently, they like to go "topless at the top" even though the girls topless included their sports bras. Ah, to be young again.

On the way up to the North Peak there was so much snow melting off the trees it was like we were getting rained on. On the way down off the South Peak the trail was covered in a layer of ice. It would have been the perfect time to try out my new microspikes. But of course, I chose not to bring them. So, it was very scary and took a very long time to descend to where it was a bit less ice and more just wet. Hence, why it took almost 9 hours.

There was an awful lot of cursing and of course I blamed Dick. Knowing full well I am responsible for my own pack. When my fear factor subsided, I had to give a heartfelt apology for the cursing and the blaming.

Lesson learned – as soon as there's talk of freezing temps, micro spikes go directly into the backpack.

We took a day off hiking and I got to read the trail description for Garfield. Sounded like a good next day hike. The rest of the day was running around to check and see if the phone had shown up anywhere. First stop was back at the trailhead, nothing. Next we went to the nearest Ranger Station, they didn't have it but sent us to the police station because that's where they would have sent it anyways. At the police station they took down the description of the phone and my name and number in case someone turned it in. Which I found funny, because if they called, well, I didn't have the ability to answer.

I absolutely loved the hike up Garfield. Perhaps because of our torturous descent from the Hancocks, but the walk in the woods up Garfield felt exactly like that. A walk in the woods.

The views from Garfield were the most spectacular and I felt like we were looking out into forever. The air tasted sweeter up there somehow and anything felt possible. It is that feeling that I get from climbing a mountain in the Whites that drives me forward and never gets old.

After we finished Garfield we took another drive to the Hancocks trailhead, just in case.

The next day Dick, Sport, and I decided to hike Mount Cube before I headed back to Connecticut. We took one more drive by the Hancocks trailhead before going to the designated hike. No phone.

Mount Cube definitely felt hard. Probably because I was beat up from the Hancocks and Garfield.

My drive home made me realize how dependent I have become on my phone. I kind of got lost a couple of times, but finally made it unscathed.

First stop once I got home was to the local bookstore and I picked up an atlas.

How great the hiking community is. I was able to be in touch with Peter through messenger on the computer. A day after I'd returned to Connecticut, before going to get a new phone, I received a message from Peter saying someone called him. They had my phone and would be able to meet him since they were coming to Mystic, Connecticut for a wedding. The irony is that Mystic is the town next to where we lived. They would be there the next day. Peter met them and my phone was returned to me and unbelievably still working!

The hiking community is amazing! It was a miracle!

Though there was a happy ending for me and my phone, it was not the happy ending I'd hope for with our relationship. Our Mount Cube hike would be our last together. I really miss Sport. I did keep the Guidebooks so something good did come out of it.

PANDEMIC FOLLIES

As if having a major surgery wasn't bad enough, only a couple weeks after returning to work a bout of shingles made its way onto the scene. This was the second time it would come calling. Yes, it's as bad as they say and just to keep things interesting I became a double winner with an additional skin infection. Imagine that you put your arm in a vat of kerosene and then put a match to it. Well, that's about how my arm looked and felt.

Initially, I drove myself to the doctor's office. This was quite the sight as I couldn't stand to have anything touch my skin on my infected arm. I was able to manage getting a short sleeved shirt on. I could put my right arm in my jacket and had it draped over my left shoulder. Then drove with my left arm out the window. It was a cold day, so even though it was odd, it provided much relief. The doctor started me on antibiotics and put the idea in my head that if it got worse they might have to do surgery to save my arm.

Next morning my arm was even more swollen and I panicked. Dick was very reluctant to cancel his doctors appointments to take me to the emergency room. Thankfully, I have the best friends and

Teresa was happy to take me and stay with me. It was determined that I wasn't in immediate danger. The Emergency Room doctor said I needed to give the antibiotics a couple of days to do their job, and THEN if not better I could panic.

I had a follow up appointment with my doctor scheduled for a few days later. After three days of taking the medication and sitting with my arm held over my head, things started to look better. I was to go back to the doctor's to make sure things were improving.

My incredible girlfriends stepped up once again and had all taken turns bringing me food during another convalescence period. I decided to call upon Dick to bring dinner the night before my upcoming doctors visit. To the casual observer I'm sure it was easily identifiable that Dick should have been the one to offer, rather than I being the one to ask. It does take a lot for me to ask, but I did. He brought pizza and we enjoyed dinner and a movie.

We had a nice time, as nice a time as I could in my condition. As I was seeing him out I asked if he could take me to the doctors the next day. Since I still really couldn't stand having anything touch my skin still. He hemmed and hawed. I added that it was at the same time he walked Sport in the morning and that my doctor's office was across the street from one of Sport's favorite places to be walked.

Still more hemming and hawing Dick added that it would be hard to get Sport in the car to go.

I was aghast. I think I exclaimed, "really?"

Then he finally, as if I was twisting his arm said, "If you REALLY, REALLY need me to, I suppose I could. Do you REALLY, REALLY need me to?"

Exasperated and saddened, I answered "No, I don't REALLY, REALLY need you to."

That's when I realized that we had very different ideas of what we wanted in a partner. A couple days later he was off to visit his family for Thanksgiving. I took care of Sport while he was away. Before he left we talked about what I wanted and he said he needed to think about what he wanted. So, in conclusion, after two years and many adventures it came to light that we were each had a very different idea of what we wanted in a partnership.

We decided to break up when he returned. Seems he was interested in something far less committal or as I like to say, he just wanted a #$%& buddy.

The winter seemed a bit colder that year, but I did get to know myself better. My son, Peter, and I took a trip to Disney, our favorite thing to do together, in late February. We got to ride all the things that had been added to the park since our last trip, since we are a bit of Disney fanatics. We enjoyed going on the Millennium Falcon Smugglers Run, Avatar Flight of Passage and having breakfast at our favorite restaurant, Boma at the Animal Kingdom Lodge.

Just over two weeks after we returned home, the world shut down. We realized how incredibly lucky we were to have not contracted The COVID during the initial wave of infections. After all, we were traveling in the thick of things.

The next several months felt like we were all living through a Steven King novel. Even going to take refuge in my happy place up in the mountains was out of the question. A friend of mine passed away during that time so I gave her dog, Seamus, a new home. Seamus was a 10 year old Jack Russel and a great companion while I worked from home and maintained little interaction with the outside world. I started taking him on some local hikes.

September of 2020 I took back up on my quest to hike the Blue Blaze Trails and I wanted to complete the Appalachian Trail (AT) in Connecticut. Seamus and I started with the Nayantaquit Trail. It was nice to just go at our own pace. I had done this trail before and it seemed easier this time around even though I was woefully out of shape. Though it wasn't a huge elevation gain I was definitely struggling with my breathing during the couple of the uphills. Even without being able to breathe so well, I found that navigating my footwork was so much easier than it used to be.

The next venture for Seamus and I was to hike along the Salmon River at Day Pond State Park. This was a nice 7 mile trek, though the trail map showed 5 miles with 0.2 mi to the Day Pond Brook spur to the waterfall. This was where I took notice of the difference in the map mileage versus the my GPS APPS. I typically used both STRAVA and MapMyRun for tracking my hikes. I had been aware that my MapMyRun and STRAVA gave different readings anyways. The difference between the paper map and STRAVA seemed like a bigger discrepancy than what I noticed between the APPS.

We'd originally planned to meet up with Outdoor Doggos. We arrived at a spot only big enough for a few cars at 9:40 and waited until 9:55. I wasn't sure if we were in the right location. I didn't see any of the Outdoor Doggo people or doggos, so we decided to go ahead. I'm always slow anyways and figured they'd catch up to us. It was probably better we went alone so that we could go at our own pace and I enjoyed having Seamus all to myself. We never did see the Outdoor Doggos crew but we had a delightful time none the less. Getting to have the waterfalls all to ourselves was an unexpected added bonus.

Seamus, I must say was in his element. He was a funny little thing, very distinguished looking. He always looked like he was going to start a conversation on the proper use of the semicolon. At home he would play fetch, well, until you just couldn't throw anymore. He didn't have that extra nervous energy that you associate with Jack Russell, eager to chase that ball, but never nervous.

The following week I reached out to Linda, whom I used to hike with when I was with Dick, to see if she wanted to join me on a hike.

After about a year away from the White Mountains, I was getting myself in shape to attempt a 4000 Footer. From what I understood Sleeping Giant would provide an excellent training ground.

I was delighted that Linda had joined Seamus and I. We decided to meet in the afternoon around 2:00 pm. I was able to get off work early and figured we'd get done before dark. We took the White Trail out. Which ended up being a perfect training trail. There were several rocky scrambles. I had studied the trail map before we went in order to find the best lookout spots to hit early, just in case it did start to get dark before we finished.

On the rocky scrambles I did need to pick up Seamus which he did not appreciate. The three miles we traveled on the White Trail took three hours. Though we didn't gain much in elevation, adding the scrambles did help with seeing how fit, or unfit I was, and gave me an idea of pace I could expect for my upcoming trip. We took the Yellow Trail Back which was essentially a smooth dirt road, so made it in just over an hour.

Lesson learned was that the maps don't jive with the tracking devices and each app doesn't match any other app navigation system when it comes to mileage. Since I'm not in a position to threaten any speed records, I'm pretty content with all the discrepancies. From that day on I decided to use mileage for planning purposes only. If expecting an over four mile day, have a full lunch and extra water packed. The days I'm hiking, that's my plan, to hike. I enjoy my surroundings. See what there is to see and immerse myself in the experience.

FIRST SOLO HIKE IN THE WHITES

The week after the training hike and more than a year from the last visit to the Whites it was time to return to New Hampshire. Even though I was able to rent a hotel room the pandemic was still dictating our isolation. When signing into the hotel I had to verify that I hadn't been around anyone that was known to have had the COVID virus for up to two weeks and that I myself wasn't exhibiting any symptoms for up to two weeks prior to my visit. At that time I was still working from home and Linda was the only one that I'd seen for that time period.

Things were weird in the lobby. I felt like what I imagine a ghost town in the old wild west was like when all the occupants had suddenly decided to leave. Eerily still and just a person behind a plexiglass wall to greet you. You could see that they were afraid of getting too close even though there was an invisible wall between us. We were still in the "mask-up" and prior to the vaccine coming out phase. At least the mountains were "open" again. We had finally come through the period of time that AMC declared that summits would not be counted to help keep people from traveling to NH and to help with efforts of containing the spread of the virus.

Prior to the lockdown I had become a member of several FB groups that provided great information on where to get updates regarding weather, trail conditions, and general questions. The two pages that I started with are *The 4,000 Footer Club-Climbing and Hiking in New Hampshire* and *Hike the 4000 footers of NH!* From them I learned about the mountain forecast website (www.mountain-forecast.com) to check conditions on specific peaks. This is the one I use the most often and find it a pretty good indicator of what's happening on the peaks. I still am only comfortable with accuracy with a 24 hour window. For the higher peaks, especially in the Presidential Range I rely on information from Mount Washington. This can be found on the Mount Washington Observatory page at www.mountwashington.org.

The plan was to hike Mount Cardigan, a 52WAV, as a warmup on Saturday and if all went well, then tackle Mount Moosilauke one of the 4,000 Footers. I had checked the weather on mountain forecast before leaving Connecticut and conditions looked favorable. I didn't feel the need to check the Mt Washington for the higher peak forecast. Nowhere did I see snow show up, but sure enough, after I checked into my hotel it started snowing. The updated mountain forecast page added a chance for snow overnight. And snow there was come morning. It was the first snow of the season and I decided to go for it.

I'd actually become quite obsessed with reading various stories of predicaments encountered in the White Mountains. The books *Where You'll Find Me, Desperate Steps, Not Without Peril,* and *Following Atticus* made a huge impact on me. All of them instilled in me the necessity of constant self-evaluation that has become part of my hiking ritual.

After reading those books I learned to be prepared for anything and I did have my extra layers knowing that people could die of exposure any time of the year in the Whites. I also had my spikes, because I knew there was potential for stuff freezing and coming down the Hancocks on icy rocks will forever be burned into my memory.

I relied that day on my All Trails App since the White Mountain map I chose to bring didn't go that far south and I hadn't downloaded a papr copy of Mount Cardigan. I also failed to bring my 52WAV book so I didn't have the trail information regarding snow. Because it was the first snow of the season, the trail reports on All Trails didn't mention any snow and the last report indicated that this was a good choice. I ended up picking the Mount Cardigan Loop Trail. I took the loop counterclockwise, even though the recommended route is clockwise.

The trail starts going up right away so I found myself laboring right out of the gate. I passed one person who was on their way down. I didn't put on my spikes since the snow was only about four inches when I started, soft and sticky. As the sun warmed the treetops, the snow started melting and it began to drop in clumps. I was in a snowball fight with the trees and the trees were winning. The raining snow clumps continued the whole time I was in the woods. So, when I got to the old fire cabin (which is an AMC cabin) I was completely soaked pack and all.

I followed the footsteps from the man I passed, and though I didn't encounter anyone else on my way up, following footsteps, even if they were going in the opposite direction gave me some comfort. Just past the cabin I looked up and saw only open ledge in front of me. I knew if I decided to continue up, that there was no going back this way. As the snow had been melting away, there were bare spots of rock exposed. Those spots provided surprisingly good grippiness under my feet. There were other areas that were all covered in snow and at those times I found that crawling on my hands and knees was the only way to go. Besides being completely soaked I also became exhausted. While climbing on my hands and knees, it did occur to me that I could sit on one of the "dry" spots and just start blowing my whistle.

Thankfully, All Trails was good about showing where I was. I was not only able to see that I was still on the right track, I knew that the trail I'd be taking on the descent was almost close enough to see. And with every step I was closer to the summit. That was enough for me to keep trudging, crawling, and trouncing my way forward. My greatest fear at that point was if I was to start sliding, how would I stop?!?!?! It was just a rock slab for about a half mile!

Then like magic after the steepest scariest section the fire tower just appeared. Big as life. That of course was when the wind decided to have its fun with me. But I was more determined than it was strong. And even though I got nearly knocked off my feet, I snapped a selfie, hunkered down and pushed forward to tag it. Anyways, at the time there was no reason to post that or tell my friends or Peter since they worried enough about me.

Don't you know on the way down I didn't go a step without seeing someone else on the trail. I was just scared enough after that experience to not solo again for quite a while.

When I got home I pulled out my 52WAV book, and read the passage about the Holt Trail and how it was the most difficult trail on the mountain and should never be attempted when wet or icy. I thought surely that must have been the trail I was on.

Two and a half years later I'd go up Cardigan with some hiking buddies, Nancy and Stacy, and learn that I was not on the Holt trail after all. I had gone up South Ridge Trail to Clark Trail and even though the open ridge section is just over a quarter mile, it still felt like a half mile to me. Nancy, Stacy and I went up the West Ridge

Trail and had planned to do the same loop I had done, but clockwise. However, once on the top of the mountain we looked down Clark and it looked every bit as scary as I remember. We opted to NOT attempt it.

After returning home from the second Cardigan summit, I went back through the 52WAV book. There was no description about the Clark Trail and I likely would have found myself in the same predicament regardless.

Needless to say, Moosilauke would have to wait for another day. Instead, I used my atlas to navigate home and took all the less travelled roads. That in itself was quite an adventure. Sometimes it's nice to just unplug and see where the road takes you.

FIRST HIKING BUDDIES HIKE

Another year would go by before I would make my way back up to my beloved mountains. Many life events had taken place. In July I'd spent the month in Florida helping my mother during an illness. It had been over a year since anyone had been to visit her and much needed to be done. That led me to evaluate my own situation. With a house much grander than I required and stuff galore it was time to start down sizing. As soon as I returned home I started purging.

The housing market soared and I figured, what the hell, lets see what it's worth. When the realtor dropped the magic number that she thought we could list it for, I said go for it. Within 30 minutes of the listing going live I had someone walking through the house. Me, my stuff, and my recently acquired feral cats needed somewhere to go. A friend, well, the one who had provided two of the three cats offered to let me rent her home.

By October I was moved and continued the purging process. One carload at a time off to Goodwill. Yet there was still so much stuff. As Thanksgiving approached I found that the job I used to love to go to became harder and harder to go to. The first 17 years there I absolutely loved going to work. One bad boss spoiled the following 8 years. After numerous job re-locations within the company it was time for me to raise the white flag and surrender. I took an early retirement and have not regretted that decision for a second.

Christmas was coming and I didn't want to be sitting around feeling sorry for myself. I'd joined the Hiking Buddies NH48 Facebook page before the pandemic and had signed up for a couple hikes that were canceled due to weather. Since then, I'd been a voyeur on the page. When I saw a Christmas hike listed for Pierce, I jumped on.

I drove up Christmas Eve and the host texted whether I'd still hike in the snow since I was coming from so far. I answered that I was good with the snow since the forecast was only going to be a couple of inches. On my drive to the trailhead, which was only a 15 minute drive a flurry of messages started pinging on my phone. By the time I pulled into the parking lot at the AMC Highland Center, the host had canceled the hike. She did say that there was someone else there. Sure enough there was one other person bumping around the car in the lot. I got myself ready and go approach Rich. I asked if he was Rich, he answered yes. In retrospect I should have asked his name instead. He said that he was planning on hiking something that day. So, I asked if I could tag along.

I felt like I hit the jackpot since he had lots of experience and I had little winter hiking in The Whites. The conversation just seemed to flow. It was like walking in a winter wonderland. We were presented with a winter wonderland made possible by Mount Pierce and some of the heavenly white stuff. What a great day. I was hooked on The Whites dressed in white.

I felt the Christmas magic and thought it was going to be a Hallmark Movie Ending. And it was, just that the romance happened between me and the mountains instead of the man. It only took me a year and a half to realized that he wasn't quite the person he represented himself as. But by the time I realized that I was hooked on Hiking Buddies and that has made all the difference. Many friendships have been forged and I don't regret that one bit.

A NEW YEAR AND
A HIKING WE WILL GO

Hikerbabes is an excellent group for women who are looking to hike with others. I had joined the Connecticut, Rhode Island, and Southern New Hampshire chapters. My favorite thing was that they did hikes during the weekdays and provided hikes much more accessible to me. We had a very wet start to the year so I jumped at joining a hike in Rhode Island. I enjoyed hiking the Ben Utter Trail with a wonderful group of ladies from the Hikingbabes Rhode Island chapter. It was good to get out in between the deluges.

Mid-January I decided to give hosting a hike a try through one of the Connecticut hiking pages. The plan was to hike at Cockaponset State Park. It was about a half hour drive for me, finally something more local that I'd been wanting to do anyway. It seemed prudent to actually know what the trail was like before showing up and going with a group. I printed out my trail maps, made sure I had my 10 essentials and off on my scouting mission. This would be my first solo hike since the Cardigan debacle.

TORTOISE TREKKER ADVENTURES

On the scouting mission I decided to take the blue trail to the yellow trail that went up and around the reservoir. From there I picked up red/blue that ended on a cliff. These were the type of things that were good to find out before having others follow along. Backtracked and found where the red/blue trail intersected with white trail. Started on the white trail but it looked like it headed in the wrong direction. Back to intersection and found the yellow/white trail headed in correct direction. This led to the yellow trail and there were so many turns that it looked like a drunk was let loose in the woods with a can of paint and said, find your way out and mark your way while you do. I was literally saying what the #%$@?

The next day was the scheduled hike. I felt good about what trail was what as I showed up at the parking area across from the trailhead. Though it looked like a couple of people had confirmed online, no one showed up. I took the opportunity to do a shorter hike from the blue to white trail loop. I knew it was a long shot that others would be able to go on a weekday after all.

There was a hike posted in Hiking Buddies for Carter Dome and since it was a 48er that I still needed I went ahead and signed up. Nancy was hosting and I liked that Nancy reached out to everyone that was signed up to make sure it wasn't their first time hiking a 4000 Footer. She had made snowshoes a requirement since we were going up in the winter. That led me on a journey to find a pair before heading up.

The day before heading up I took a drive to EMS, but they had been downsizing even before the pandemic began and were out of any snowshoes my size. On my way up to New Hampshire I was off to Dicks Sporting goods where I FINALLY found someone who reluctantly helped me. When I explained my predicament, his attitude changed and he became super helpful. We walked over to where the snowshoes had been and decided that the few there wouldn't fit the bill for what I wanted to do. He made a call up to the Hartford store, which was perfect since it was on my way North, or at least I could make it so. There was no time to lose as the store would be closing just about the time I could make it up there. What a delight when I arrived at the Hartford store because the first person I met happened to be who my helpful Dick's representative had talked to an hour earlier. They had exactly what we asked for and I would be able to meet up for the hike fully prepared.

The next morning I made it to the trailhead nice and early. After meeting Nancy we decided the trail was packed down enough to start in spikes but we should carry our snowshoes. I used my paracord and just tied the shoes around my pack. Nancy showed how she used flexible cable ties and said she'd tried all kind of methods including the popular bungie cords that many hikers use. I was still using my summer pack, since that was the only one I had. I had made a water bottle holder to attach to my shoulder strap because I did not want to use my water bladder when temps dropped below freezing. Other than that my pack was busting at the seams.

I made it up a couple miles when my lungs decided that they had enough of going uphill and went on strike. Even a toke on the trusty old inhaler was not enough to abate the wheezing. Though I did not make the summit, the company and the journey up my beloved Nineteen-Mile Brook trail were worth the trip.

Nancy suggested that I stop by Mount Willard since the day was young and it was on my way home. So, I headed onto another great adventure. Not before spotting my potential new home, the tiny little maintenance shack nestled in the bosom of the woods beside the Nineteen-Mile Brook.

A bit of a drive and I was at the train station adjacent to the AMC Highland Center. I fueled up with a pb&j, thermos full of hot cocoa-coffee, then back on the trails. Ah, then slog, wheeze, gasp for air, stop to look around at the beauty of nature wondering if anyone else could hear my heartbeat. It rang through my eardrums drowning out all other sound, breathing returned to normal and outside sounds are heard once again, repeat...

Along the way I was "greeted" by a series of dogs and their mostly ill behaved humans. Bitten once, okay, to be fair, that was back on the Nineteen-Mile Brook trail and my mistake for having pet him as I slipped off the trail. While heading up the trail to Willard I was barked at multiple times by the same dog. Note to owners, please understand the difference between aggressive and playful barking. Honestly, I don't care if you think they are friendly, I may not be. I was approached by several more canines that came up to me before the owners even knew I was there. I'd love to give the "keep your dogs on a leash or leave them at home" speech, but I know that each owner thinks their dog is more entitled to their liberties than I am my safety and solitude on the trail.

So, you may ask why bother? My little digital photos will never be able to capture the magic that happens. To be humbled by such enormity, the beauty, the changing of the flora as one changes elevation, the sound of running water beneath the ice or the ice as it cracks and shifts sometimes feeling like it's your own spine cracking, are just a few of the reasons. Something is transformative each and every time I explore a new trail or reach a new summit, or even bail before the summit. Take the time to play outside and free your soul, you will not be sorry.

THE LONGEST DAY EVAH!!!

Nancy posted another hike, this time to Owl's Head. Now, there are three hikes that I wanted to get done so they didn't end up on my "Final" list. They were Owl's Head, Isolation, and the Bonds (Three 4000 Footers in one hike). These I consider the long and hard ones. I knew that Owl's Head wasn't necessarily difficult but extremely long.

The normal route up Owl's Head is listed as 18 miles. In the winter about a mile is cut off by using the Brutus Bushwack.

I sent Nancy a message asking if she minded if I joined knowing that I couldn't make it up to Carter Dome. She said that I had proven myself even if I hadn't made it to the summit. Sometimes knowing when to turn back was even more important. We met early in the morning with five of us geared up and ready to take on this arduous journey. I had run three marathons and two ragnars by this time so I figured that a 17 mile hike should be doable in a day.

The following is my post-hike review. Largely as it was written on Facebook. I did edit it to help make it a little more reader friendly.

2/9/22 - Owl's Head (11/48)

Nancy, Charleen, Bill, Kaios, and James

Started 7am ended 10:30pm - My app said 10.3 mi to summit. Almost 20 miles with approximately 3000' elevation gain, according to my STRAVA.

Thank you Nancy Hall for setting up the Hiking Buddies group! See below for the rest of the story...

Owl's Head on Wednesday via Brutus (or should I say Brutal) Bushwack. Thanks to all who were there from beginning to end or joined for just a while. Not for the faint of heart for sure.

First, a shout out to the Hiking Buddies NH 48 that participated in this epic adventure. There was our fearless leader Nancy Hall, with first time to Hiking Buddies Charleen (not her first time tackling a 4000 Footer though), Bill (stuck with the slow crew the whole way), Kaios (started with us), James (showed up when we (and when I say we, I mean I) needed him most).

We started with five of us a little after 7:00 am. Conditions at the start were pretty good, we all started with microspikes. About one and a half miles in a few of us opted to switch to snowshoes, myself included. The trail was broken out, but personally I found it easier in the snowshoes, because it helped my stride and I felt more balanced. Going was good for the first seven miles or so, then things warmed up and the snow began to stick, adding weight to each step.

As we approached the Brutal Bushwack, James caught up to us. He started two hours after us, but was there when it truly mattered. As I was doing my best to make headway it seemed that for every step forward, I would end up sliding two steps back down. The snow would give way in sheets, partially due to my snowshoes acting as shovels, compacting sections that would give way. After sliding back down 40 feet or so, with Nancy as my backstop, I switched back to microspikes. Then the clumping made that a futile effort and Bill came to the rescue. He had serious mountaineering snowshoes which he offered up for the cause. James stayed behind and talked, guided, and provided encouragement to get us all to the summit. So very grateful for the help.

If James hadn't been there I'm sure I would have decided to bail, as I have done on previous hikes, and I never regretted it. That day, as slow as I was going I felt I could recover enough at the top and come down safely. Summit we did, I used my semi-adequate snowshoes for the descent. We tried hard not to butt slide but shit happens. Bill patiently followed behind and did his best to clean up the trail from all our slipping and sliding. The temps had dropped before our descent and the snow became decent.

Onward and trudgingly, the final four, as we lost one group member before the summit, then released James due to his valiant efforts getting us all safely to the summit, donned our headlamps and marched on, and on, and on...

Personally, about a hundred times in my mind as we slogged the final five miles, I wanted to just curl up in my bivvy sack and be done. Instead, Bill mentally pushed me from behind as I used imaginary cords tied to Nancy and Charleen to drag me onward. You two women were beasts!

We reached our vehicles around 10:30 pm.

That was the hardest thing I've ever done, physically anyway.

Thank God it is done.

In hindsight it may have been the hardest thing mentally that I've done as well. Don't know when else I've had to dig that dep to just keep putting one foot in front of the other. We never got off our feet and 17.5 hours is the longest time I've ever been on my feet and I vow to never let that happen again. My feet still aren't right over two years later.

LAFAYETTE AT LAST

It was so exciting to see a Hiking Buddies event for Lafayette. Finally, a chance to tackle the summit that I sought on my first trip to The White Mountains. All healed up, I headed back to the North Country. An added benefit was that Stacy was hosting and I revered her. She sounded awesome and was a self-proclaimed curser (as in swear words, not writing style). I always enjoy a good cursing. Some feel the need to justify it by saying "she works in a shipyard" but those that know me and love me for who I am understand that it's just part of my DNA. I've actually tried to control it and that only seems to cause me to bubble up those %$@! even more.

We had a nice intimate group of four on a beautiful March day. Which meant that it was still wintertime and a nice packed out trail to follow. Though the sign at the start of the trail stated 4.0 miles to Lafayette my STRAVA recorded 8.96 miles with us completing in just under 9 hours. Establishing that we were indeed turtle paced hikers.

This was my FB review.

3/10/22 – Lafayette (12/48)
Stacy, Eugenia, Al
Dist 8.96 mi Elev gain 3,583 ft Time 8:58:46
Yes, it is the long awaited post Mount Lafayette hike review from yesterday's achievement.

Another incredible day up in The Whites with another incredible Hiking Buddies' crew. I will embellish later but here's a few of the pics and little video I shot up at the Greenleaf Hut.

Not very exciting, and, no, I never went back later to embellish, so I'll do my best to do that now. After the Owl's Head report I think I was feeling pressure, if only from myself, to do a similar write-up and therefore turned into over analysis paralysis.

I started in snowshoes, but the trail was really too hard packed for them so after about a mile and a half I followed suit with everyone else and switched to micro spikes. Shortly after that we ran into a woman who had turned back. She told us of an icy cascade spot that even with crampons she didn't feel comfortable attempting. We were all a bit freaked out but decided to continue on and make a decision as to whether to turn back once we assessed the situation. When we came upon the ice flow, we initially had the same reaction as the woman we encountered. Having buddies gave us more freedom to consider options and Eugenia found a way around by making a bushwack and we got past the first scary spot.

Luckily, we had a respite at the Greenleaf Hut which was just past our adventurous bushwack. Onward and upward to where it was above tree line and by far a much scarier place to be. There was pretty much a sheet of ice covering the open ledges and if you start sliding you could just slide right off the mountain. With this in mind, as it goes up there was a couple with a dog. The woman was even more freaked out than I was. They were coming down as we were going up. The woman was just saying "I can't, I can't, I can't."

The guy had the dog and let it go just as I came around the corner. Well, the dog was very excited and come bounding down to greet me as I was plodding along. For a hot minute I thought he was going to jump up and send me off into the abyss. To my relief the dog stopped short and just bounced up and down in front of me. I was finally able to breathe again and started picking my way back upwards. Of course, then I started to worry about the coming down.

Ahhh, but reaching the summit took my breath away for another reason. The views were spectacular and the fear of what lay ahead vanished. After just taking it all in it was time to return from whence we came.

Good news was that on our way down the couple was no longer there, so the woman did indeed make it. Even though the fear had started to return this fact brought some relief. Thankfully hiking with Stacy we did go toe to toe with the curse words during our descent. That was another great relief and I knew I'd found my people. With the two of us in a cursing concert we made it back down the icy platform at the summit. Plus, the sun had warmed the ice enough so we had some good grip on the way off the ledge. Yes, there is a thing such as skicky ice, or at least less slippery ice.

Coming back through the coniferous forest after the heart pounding escape from the ledges was such a treat. And as if things couldn't get any more delightful by magic the Greenleaf Hut appears. Our own little safe haven to rest up and reflect. We contemplated sun bathing but it was just a tad too chilly for that. We determined that our outdoor bathroom spot around the side of the Hut afforded the best potty break viewpoint in The Whites.

We stopped to enjoy the view of Lafayette, The Franconia Ridge, and Lincoln from the open ledge before getting to the ice flow. Al had crampons and made it down without much issue and proceeded to help the rest of us. Eugene went down the bypass we'd all taken to get up around the frozen waterfall, but that looked scarier to me rather than going down the icefall. The first part of the ice cascade had turned mostly into mashed potatoes and the bottom part had some rocks that I used to wedge myself between. So, I just forged ahead and to Stacy's disbelief I went down the ice cascade.

The rest of the way down was smooth sailing. Another successful Hiking Buddies hike in the books. And a reminder about what we can do together.

YOSEMITE BOUND

Next up was a trip to Yosemite. I'd signed up before deciding to retire. This had been a bucket list item for me. Actually visiting the National Parks in general. In order to help get myself in shape I'd signed up for the Yosemite Half Marathon. There was a fundraiser that raised awareness of Environmental Education so of course I tacked that onto my challenge. As I did my fundraiser pleading I'd give some updates on my training.

On 4/24/2022 provided this FB post.

"Half marathon training check in... Practice half done. Race in less than 2 weeks. In order to be counted as complete during the race, time needs to be under 4 hours... Practice done in less than 3 1/2 hours. As long as I don't hurt myself between now and then, should be in good shape."

With several cats comes a lot of kitty litter and that gets sent in oversized boxes. The boxes would get opened at the bottom of the stairs because even with all my training lifting 60 plus pounds was never something I could do. I managed to wrestle the box inside. I was living in a raised ranch, so the box needed to go upstairs to get broken down.

Only someone with the skills that I have can fall going upstairs carrying one of the said boxes. Don't you know as I was falling I just assumed the box would collapse and provide some cushioning. Instead I was amazed at the fortitude and craftsmanship as my full weight slammed into the edge and I'm not sure but I may have heard a cracking sound. As I bounced up all I could think was "don't fall backwards" so I rolled to the side and wedged myself against the stairs railing. As I was overcome with pain, there was a wave of relief that I didn't get launched back down the stairs, and a small amount of admiration thinking perhaps the box could be made into a coffee table. Not really sure how I managed to un-wedge myself.

My ribs were definitely bruised and I thought possibly cracked. That took running off the table for the next few days. So much for being on track with my training. Also made travelling a joy. I did try running a week before the race, just to see if I could. That was when I realized that it was not only my ribs and breathing that was affected, but I'd also hurt one of my quads. Needless to say but I was a tad concerned about whether I would be able to complete the run.

Note to self never say "…as long as I don't hurt myself…" Good old self sabotage.

It's funny that the question I get asked most about taking a two week trip to Yosemite is still "by yourself?" It's not really in the form of a question but more of an exclamation of disbelief. In some ways I suppose I'd felt as if someone should be sharing the experience with me. Now I know it's anyone who chooses to read about my escapades. I felt oddly comfortable planning the trip for myself alone perhaps because I really enjoy my own company.

It was quite liberating. I have traveled often, for work, for play, to visit family, so that was familiar to me. What was different was that since graduating from college my trips usually involved others, friends, co-worker, family or sweethearts. And though this was a solo trip I never felt alone. Until 9/11 happened I always loved the travelling part.

When I made the plans for the trip I was still working. When I retired at the beginning of the year, I had budgeted for this trip knowing it would be the only big trip that year. So, flights, hotel, rental car, food and any extra activities including guided hikes took a bite out of my savings. It started me in my new retiree mode, thou I didn't really deny myself anything yet. I did become more mindful of my spending and booked my stay at the Wawona Lodge and chose a room with a shared bathroom to help economize.

Being at the Wawona Hotel seemed a fitting place to stay. It was very exciting to go to a place with so much history and I felt propelled back in time. It is perhaps the most economical luxury spot. I wanted a place that was in the park but nearby the half marathon. Even though the half marathon is called Yosemite Half Marathon it isn't actually in the park.

Driving up to the majestic National Landmark, where I was staying, was like taking a step back in time. It was beautiful and breathtaking. The large verandas for each building gave a welcoming feeling. They spoke to weary travelers saying, 'come, sit, take a load off, forget your troubles and relax'. Because of the shared bathroom situation I thought of it as a very high class glamping affair. Much like in many campgrounds there was a camp, grocery, and souvenir shop with a post office all rolled into one located next to the hotel.

The first thing that made it clear that we were in a national forest was based on the info on the form that you were required to sign upon check-in. It raised ones alert system that you had to sign a form when you checked in stating that it is illegal to leave any food in your vehicle due to bears. In the park itself there were bear boxes and at the hotel you had your room. This made things real, exciting, and a bit frightful.

The first day was a long one and I was ready to have a bite to eat before I entered the hangry state. There was a restaurant at the hotel but the day I checked in they said the restaurant was not taking any more reservations for that evening. Leaving me in a bit of a bind since the store would be closing before I could get there to grab some food. The hotel clerk assured me that I shouldn't have a problem getting into the restaurant for any other dinners for the rest of my stay there as long as I was there before 5pm since the extra openings were on a first come first serve situation.

I had noticed the Tenaya Lodge on my drive in so took a chance that they'd have an opening in their restaurant. So glad I did because the Jackalope's Bar & Grill was perfect. I had an amazing meal and it didn't break the bank.

When I got back to Wawona I posted on FB, 'Home Sweet Home for the next week plus.' Complete with a smiley face, sun between two mountains, and a runner emoji.

Back to the Wawona and ready to call it a day. "Climbing" into my bed was near impossible due to my hurting ribs. I had to jump in kind of like a fish, head first with my arms at my side then flop and twist myself into position. When I finally maneuvered myself into place realized that the walls were paper thin. I could hear absolutely everything in the room next door. I was just grateful that it wasn't a newlywed couple on their honeymoon.

I slept like a baby.

YOSEMITE HALF MARATHON ANTICS

I found it interesting and a bit disappointing that the person who checked me in and others working the desk had no idea that there was a half marathon, where it was, or any information about it. The only place that had internet service was in the "sun" room of the hotel. So, the first thing on my agenda was to pull up the email with information on registration. Okay, second thing. First thing was to get to the store after breakfast and stock up on some food for the week. I did make it to the Wawona restaurant for breakfast that morning but knew that it wouldn't open early enough for the next day and I'd need something before the race. I did make it to the store and I was hoping to just do yogurt and granola, foiled again, no yogurt! I'd just have to make do with granola bars. While in Rome…

I was able to get the information from my email on where the registration and race start was. After finding my way to registering and checking out the final mile or so of the race I was able to hit my new favorite restaurant for lunch. Then headed to the Mariposa Grove.

I knew I only had a short bit of time so my hike was really just the walk, test my Garmin Mini2 and maybe make it to the grove itself.

About a month before the trip I knew it was time to purchase a satellite tracking device. Since I knew I would be doing some solo hiking and wanted to put my friends' and family's minds at ease. I chose the Garmin Mini2. It's been one of the best purchases to date. I used it mainly to send a link to a few people when I hike solo and check in when I've reached a milestone or mountain summit, then let them know when I've returned to the car.

With its maiden voyage under my belt I'd get a chance to put my Garmin through its paces over the next several days. I always carry it with me on hikes. On group hikes I rarely send a link out during those times since I'm with others. However, I do let the others who hike with me know that it has an SOS button if someone needs to use it.

What can I say about the Yosemite Half marathon? It was beautiful though I wasn't able to get any pics, so you'll just have to take my word for it.

It was 2:30 am, the alarm on the phone began to chime. All my race stuff was ready, I dressed, and had a bite for breakfast. I skipped to the car (okay, maybe not skip, but I was a little excited).

I made it to the shuttle pickup location by 4:00 am. The bus ride to the start was about 45 minutes and lucky for me there was a port-a-potty right there at the bus stop. I had briefly thought about putting my phone in my fanny pack before heading in to do my business. But I wanted to get in and out quick because the line for the bus was getting long fast. So, I set the phone on the toilet paper holder, thinking "it's flat enough."

That would be the first critical error of the day. The phone started to slide, but I was already mid drawer drop so all I could do was cry out "no, no, noooooo..."

But yes, it did, 'kerplunk', right into the pungent emerald blue abyss. I was helpless as I heard the distinct plop. It was too dark to see, so I hastily pull up my shorts, swing open the door, and in a panic asked a fellow runner to shine a light. Maybe, just maybe it was saved by something somewhat solid?!?!

And that my friends is why there are no race photos. It did not stop me from enjoying the race. I don't really know if it made up for losing my phone, but there was coffee upon arrival at the starting area. The slow folks got to start first which was so great, we usually go last resulting in waterless water stops.

I was hoping to finish the half marathon in under the four hour time limit. However, once I started I was feeling pretty good and my quad loosened up and my breathing remained un-wheezy. A 3 hrs and 30 minutes overall time would have made me happy. I was ecstatic at a total time of 3 hours, 12 minutes, and 53 seconds. This may have a bit to do with the fact that the race was all downhill. I should run more downhill races.

With the race over it was time to board a bus, get to my car, and on to purchase a new phone. Well, without a phone to help me out there was another adventure just waiting to happen. You would have thought that I learned to keep paper maps at least in the car after the phone loss on the Hancocks. But it's true, I still haven't learned that lesson.

Anyways, the half marathon ended at Bass Lake. Race organizers had busses ready to take folks back to the car spots. There were several stops and I of course got off at the wrong one. I knew not to get off at the Best Western because we'd picked up there after our spot. I'd parked at the high school but hadn't really paid attention to the landmarks at 4 am. You'd think I would have remembered the fated port-a-potty with my phone swimming at the bottom of it. That was pretty memorable, even at 4:00 AM.

A couple stops en route we came to a school, and well, all the school buildings looked pretty much the same. They were all tan colored and manufactured units. I got off the bus and though the buildings looked similar I didn't recognize an area that looked like where I parked. Then thought that the road started to look familiar so started walking and that maybe the area ahead was where I parked. Only after I approached the lot I realize that it wasn't the one.

I headed back towards the area that I was dropped off and noticed a pet store on the corner. I decided to go in and asked where the high school was. It was a mile down the adjacent road. So, what's an extra couple miles walk after a half marathon? Just a nice cool down.

As I headed towards the correct school, I saw a couple other people walking past me in the other direction. We chatted and I found out because they also got off at the wrong stop, and that felt oddly comforting. They were parked at the school that I disembarked the bus from. After locating my car, I drove to the pet store hoping they could give me directions to the nearest Verizon Store, since they were so helpful getting me to my car.

Back at Steve's Pet shop I told my tale of woe and the port-a-potty folly. The person at the register said just turn left and you'll see the plaza with the grocery store, make sure you go in there and not into the CVS parking lot. You'll find the Verizon Store there. Sure, it sounded simple enough. So, back from where I came and turned left at the first intersection, though a little voice in my head said "maybe it's the next one."

I think he thought I knew that the main road was the second intersection, I did not…

I chose to ignore the little voice and we were on Rt-425B. And after a while, even without a map, or a phone, I realized that we were not on the right road. Therefore, I kept making left turns thinking eventually we'd just make a loop if nothing else. And before I knew it, well, really after quite a drive actually, we were back at Bass Lake but not near the race. I just drove around the lake until I came upon a little resort nestled along the shore. The we here would be me and that little voice that I choose to ignore more times than not.

Ah, civilization at last. In the little camp store I asked the girl at the counter if she happened to have a map of the area. She proceeded to produce a simple map of the Lake area. I asked if she could tell me where we were on the map. She just looked at me with those big doe eyes and pointed to the back of the store, where there was a queue of people lined up through the store. She said to see the woman in the back. "Marie can help you. I don't really know where we are on the map."

I didn't have anywhere else to be so I took my place in line and waited my turn to talk to Marie. It was a small store and most every-one in there was waiting to talk to Marie. Marie apparently took care of everything that was not just a grab and pay for item. There were ski-doo rentals, camp spot check-ins, boat rentals, and resort check-ins. Each of these required forms to be filled out, waivers, liabilities, explanation of what to do and where to go, how to get to spots or return their items and by what time.

Finally, it was my turn. Within a few seconds she had circled where we were on the map. She drew arrows where to go and where to turn cautioning about one of the tricky intersections and ex-plained that I wanted to make sure not to turn too soon. Then last, but not least, she put a box on the map and labeled the store at my destination. I surely hope that she makes more than minimum wage. To anyone else who may need to hear this, if you work at a resort perhaps you should know where you're located on the maps that you will hand out.

Since I had to drive all the way around the Lake to get to where I wanted to go, I found a nice little open park along the way with public restroom and picnic table beside the Lake to stop and enjoy the snack pack provided by the race people. That seemed to make the whole side trip worth it and seemed to have gotten lost for a beautiful reason.

Note to self, remember to listen to that little voice...

YOSEMITE HIKES AND SIGHTS

Planning is one of my very favorite things to do. Maps, guide-books, websites, google are all my friends. For this trip I used 'Yosemite – The Complete Guide Book' to help focus on what I didn't want to miss. I really wanted to give Half Dome a whirl but the fixed lines weren't up for the season, so couldn't even register in the lottery. No Half Dome for me, at least on that visit. Who knows what the future holds?

Part of my planning included arranging guided hikes as well as some solo exploring. The day after the half marathon just happened to be Mother's Day. I treated myself to my first guided hike down in the valley. With my new phone I was ready for some awesome photo opportunities. My first time driving into the valley down the windy mountain roads was nerve wracking. I was white knuckle driving and too terrified to admire how beautiful the views were. Luckily there were plenty of pull offs to let those that weren't gripping their steer-ing wheel and praying for a safe arrival on their descent, pass.

Having survived the mountain road drive, I come through the Wawona Tunnel and was greeted with the most amazing view and the Ah factor begins. It seems like you will drive right into Brid-alveil Falls as it looms in front of you. Continuing on as El Capitan make an up-close and personal appearance, was absolutely breath-taking.

I had recently watched 'Free Solo', the movie, and imagining any-one scaling the rock face in general was beyond my imagination, much less to do it without any safety equipment still seems insane to me. I imagined how my brother must have felt, for I know that he has climbed El Cap and continued climbing all around the world. He went on to make that his life work for a while.

We met with our guide, Andrew, at the Yosemite Lodge. There was a little amphitheater where a couple of people were hanging out. There ended up being four of us plus our guide. It was perfect size. We went over the Lower Falls and enjoyed the bit of mist and a great photo op. Then through a bit of wetlands where we heard a least at least a half dozen different birds enjoying their environment. As Andrew was taking us around I thought, well, maybe I'll just stay. There was something about being out in the middle of someplace so spectacular that helped remind us of how insignificant we are. That was a beautiful thing.

Being in Yosemite we were all eager to encounter the wildlife that called this remarkable place home. One of the first things Andrew expressed to us was what to do if we did see a bear. First thing to be mindful of was a safe distance for a bear encounter. The distance can be measured by the rule of thumb which is literally using your thumb. Hold your hand up, your arm out, and make a fist and give the good old thumbs up. If you can cover up the bear with your thumb then you are far enough away. If not, do not run, or play dead, or sacrifice a slower person (for which I was thankful, because as usual, that was me), instead make yourself as big as possible. He also advised us that the use of bear spray is illegal in Yosemite.

In addition to the wildlife all of the plant life was amazing. The dogwoods were in bloom and I asked Andrew if he knew where the pink dogwood was and whether it was in bloom. I had heard that there was one in Yosemite and that a naturally occurring pink dogwood was a rare thing. I was delighted to hear that he did know where it was and told me where I could find it.

I expressed how wonderful it would be to just stay and work at the park, so Andrew explained how his parents were volunteers for the national forest and would provide stewardship at different parks. This sounded ideal to me, except, I am a bit more greedy and want to do that but get paid. It was then that I decided that I indeed would be heading back to the East Coast after all.

Our trek took us to the foot of El Capitan where we happily enjoyed our lunch. Talk about humbling, it did take my breath away. After eating we looked for climbers. We did spot a couple of them, they weren't much more than a dot on the wall. We also spotted a few portaledges, which are the suspended platforms for hikers camping on the side of El Cap. They were sooooo tiny, which meant they were way up high.

After the hike I did a quick drive by the field that I thought the pink dogwood was, but the field was immense, and I didn't really know where to look. I continued on to the Ahwahnee where there was a very nice and maybe only sit down and get served restaurant in the valley. When I went up to the concierge to make a reservation, understanding that I might not be seated due to it being Mother's Day. I was informed that unless I was actually staying at the hotel, I could not make a reservation, or even wait on standby. And not just because it was Mother's Day. Which seemed (and still does) ludicrous to me. But really it was just another victim of the pandemic. They just didn't have the staff to man the restaurant.

After my disappointment I went to a little walk-in place behind Yosemite Lodge, The Base Camp Eatery. Though cafeteria style I was not disappointed. I ordered the Citrus Salmon Bowl and it was delightful and became my go to place when in the valley.

The next day I took a rest day. I didn't really go anywhere but just walked around the grounds, where I did a lot of napping, and had time to played my violin. Well, and tried to stay warm. I lucked out with weather for the marathon and first Valley adventure because temps were moderate and pleasant. When I woke up on my rest day I was surprised to see everything glimmering in a frosty blanket.

Remember the paper thin walls? Well, they didn't do a lot as far as insulating either. So, the rest day seemed to afford me the perfect day for snuggling back into bed and having some delicious naps in between meals and fiddling.

After getting rested up, the following day was off to Mariposa Grove. I was glad to have checked it out ahead of time so as not to be surprised about having the bit of a hike to get to the grove itself.

Another casualty of COVID was the shuttle busses that normally took people from the welcome center to the Grove Arrival Area were not running and the only those with handicapped vehicles could go up the 2 miles right to the Grove Arrival Area. I loved that I had the whole day to explore, so the extra 4 miles weren't an issue for me.

One of the main trails was blocked off with the plastic orange fencing all around the area. So a few of us pondering why, until we saw why. One of the trees had fallen right across the path. Looked like it was a fairly new path finished with pretty new wooden planks, of course.

This trek would be a solo adventure even if I wasn't alone. The main loop around the grove had so many people that it was as if the folks had come out in droves to the groves. Many of the trees were named and plaqued so I could use the map given by the park rangers so I'd know exactly where I was. Along with the crowds we came up to Bachelor and Three Graces next was Grizzly Giant. Then onto the California Tunnel Tree. After going through the tunnel the crowds thinned way out. Only a few people continued onto the upper grove. This was where I was in my glory. Me and the trees.

I came upon the Faithful Couple, two trees seemingly merged into one. Then onto the Clothespin Tree which indeed looked like an old-fashioned clothespin. On to the Mariposa Grove Cabin where I'd hoped to use the facilities. The bathrooms were closed there, so instead of continuing around the upper loop I decided to take the cut-off trail. That was where there were some fallen down trees across the path but I figured, why not, and I went over and under the ob-stacle course created by the fallen trees.

It was a nothing ventured nothing gained opportunity. Along the forbidden path I had found some of the largest pine cones I'd ever seen. So, just for the chance to see those it was worth the extra ef-fort. However, When I got to the other side of the bypass path, what were the odds that a tree would have fallen across that side too? And I couldn't get around it, since it went right into and over a water-way. There was no going under and the diameter was a good 8 ft or so. It was a challenge, but eventually I found a way over. But I was laughing because, who could have ever figured that of all the places, on literally either end of this path was blocked by trees falling per-fectly perpendicularly across the path. I was rewarded with an open restroom for my effort.

From there I decided to take the Perimeter Trail. Now the Perim-eter Trail is normally used for the horseback guided groups. But, the horses hadn't been brought back up yet, still too early in the spring. The Perimeter trail had, well, no one besides myself as far as I could tell. It was just me and the trees.

After positioning my phone just so, on one tree so that I could take a picture of myself hugging another tree. I heard something that sounded like wood splitting. Then I realized that perhaps it wasn't just me and the trees. Because I wasn't really ready to put the rule of thumb trick to the test to see if it was a bear or no bear situation. I didn't time myself but that last mile back to the lower loop may very well have been my personal best.

The next day I headed back down the windy road and much less white knuckling it as I drove down into the valley. The bike-to-hike guided tour was next on the itinerary. In order to bike-to-hike one needs to have, or in my case, rent a bike. Which was easier said than done. Upon entering the Yosemite Village there is a sign that says Bike Rentals è, so follow the arrow I did. The little path takes you to a conglomerate of bicycles with a person very ready to help, except you can't actually rent the bikes there. It was only where the bikes are kept, so back to the village entrance I went. There is a little booth at the entrance and I got in line and waited my turn. When I got to the window I asked the person in the booth if they knew any details about the bike-to-hike guided tour? Where do I meet the guide and where do I rent the bike? She said she didn't know anything about tours, since that's through the mountaineering school. So, I asked if I needed to rent a bike there and she answered, "I have no idea."

I went over to the mountaineering school, which happened to be inside the outfitter store. I asked about the tour, where to meet the guide, and the bike rental situation. They said to meet the guide out front in a half hour and that I needed to go to the booth at the entrance to rent the bike. Yes, the same booth where I asked about where I needed to go to rent a bike.

As soon as I got back to the booth the woman left out the back door saying she'd be right back. I waited there and 45 minutes later another person came back to the booth, went inside, grabbed some papers and said she had something else to do elsewhere.

Hell no, I had been sent back and forth, and then stood there for 45 minutes. Calmly but forcefully I stated, "No! You will take care of me now!"

She didn't like it, but she did it. Lo and behold, it only took 5 minutes to get me logged in and receipt for the bike. I'd like to blame that also on the pandemic. But actually, I think it was a lack of sharing basic information. If the person at the booth would have just rented me the bike when I first went up to inquire, I wouldn't have been on a wild goose chase for almost an hour.

Back to the mountaineering school and profusely apologized to Connor, my guide for the day, for making him wait. Luckily, I ended up being only a half hour later after being a half hour early. The great news was that I was the only one signed up for the bike to hike guided tour. So, I paid the group rate for my very own tour.

We biked over to Mirror Lake where I got a spectacular photo of Half Dome in the reflection. We stopped into the Conservatory Building where they showed all the programs for understanding how to help environment.

Connor showed where some of the rocks that slid off El Cap in 2017 had moved all the way to the conservation building. He happened to be in the valley and heard the crack and then saw the dust cloud.

I asked about the pink dogwood. Even though it was only three days after Andrew had told me it was in bloom the tree had past its peak, but still a thrill to see it. It was nestled in the dorm buildings where some of the workers lived.

We chatted about how it was living in the park. Connor was Andrew's roommate and it was fun to learn about life for the guides. I learned that all the workers employed by the park lived in the valley.

They start in tents with wood stoves and only after years actually moved into buildings. Still dorm style. I tried to imagine me and three semi-feral cats in a tent or shared rooms. So, poof, went my dream of staying in Yosemite and sending for the cats.

Early to bed and early to rise. The early hiker got to catch the sunrise at the tunnel view. People truly amaze me. And not always in a good way. I was probably the fifth person at the viewing area. One guy had set up his tripod already and the rest of us just tried to find a good spot to set up. I only had my phone, so yielded to those with cameras and did my best to not get in anyone's way. There were two with the tripod, then another couple.

With only a few of us there when I arrived, I felt good about getting there early. Then, as if someone announced free hot dogs at Fenway Park. Boom, there were literally people everywhere. And though I was standing in the same spot from when I first arrived, just as the sliver of light began to emerge, I started taking pictures. As I was taking pictures a woman stepped right in front of me. She stepped in the 8" between me and the stone wall. Yes, I repressed the urge to "accidentally" give her a little "nudge" and instead just took a picture of the back of her head. Thankfully her companion took her aside. I continued taking pictures as the light got brighter and the sun dazzled us and our surroundings greeting us with the magnificence of a new day, as only she can. I was drawn to the waterfall in the distance that now looked like she was spilling out in gratitude and filling the cup of happiness to all who wished to drink from it. Even the momentary inconsideration of another was washed away in the splendor before us.

With a light heart and the dazzling spectacle still shimmering before me, I found my way back to my vehicle and continued into the valley. I was delighted to see Conner again and guide-in-training Brittan. Brittan may have been a new guide to the mountaineering school but he had been in Yosemite for a few years and had plenty to share with us. This was a Discovery Hike. Besides myself there was only one other couple on the tour.

I was completely fascinated and captivated by the burn zones which I had seen on my drive in that morning and inquired about since you could smell the smoke in the air. They are controlled burns that help propagate growth, since many of the seeds need the heat in order to start the germination. I think many can relate to having to completely be stripped down to become vulnerable enough to allow new growth to form and create something wonderful.

We got to play in some caves and enjoyed learning about foraging in the park. We went to Mirror Lake again and I was able to get even better pictures than the day before. We sampled many edible plants along the way and the couple on the tour had to leave early so they took off early.

On our walk back Connor happened to look up. Brittan and I heard "Wooohhhwww!"

We asked what it was. He claimed that there was a ring around the sun. So Brittan and I exchanged glances then asked, "what were the plants that we'd sampled?"

Thinking he must surely be hallucinating. But he was insistent on saying, "no, you have to see."

So, Brittan put on his sunglasses and had the same reaction that Connor did. Honestly thinking that they were both pulling my leg, I reluctantly donned my sunglasses and took a look.

"WOW!!!!

And all three of us laughed. I asked if we "sampled" something that would make us all have the same hallucination. So, I took a picture. Sure enough it was in the photo pretty as you please, so no hallucinations after all. This halo around the sun was a perfect end to a perfect day.

Until…

I got back to the rental car and without thinking, after I unlocked the trunk, threw my backpack in, with the keys still attached to the pack and shut the trunk. Only as it latched shut had I realized that I didn't unlock the doors and now the keys were locked in the trunk.

I was truly grateful that I had reinstated my AAA membership before taking this trip and that there were pay phones still in the park. The wait for the AAA service person did give me a chance to do some shopping. I was amazed at how fast someone showed up. Then of course he tried to open the doors, but it wasn't happening. In a hail Mary effort after the AAA person said I'd need to contact the rental car company to get a set of keys brought from San Francisco. He was able to pop the trunk by squeezing his metal rod through the seats. "Whew"

The last but not least adventure was an Adventure Hike with our guide Nick. Our journey was up Mist Trail to Vernal Falls onto Nevada Falls and back down John Muir Trail. The couple from the day before was on this hike as well as one other woman. Though it's true that I am a very slow and steady type it became clear that the woman of the couple was starting to struggle. About halfway up to Vernal Falls the husband started trying to talk his bride into going back down. She didn't want to disappoint all of us and her husband. We all were in it together and we did our best to help motivate her and go at a pace that she felt comfortable. It was easy to go slow anyways because there were a ton of people all going up the rocky staircase together.

When we made it to the top of Vernal Falls we all had some lunch and just enjoyed the beauty of the raging waters. It was decided by the couple that they would not continue on. The other woman and I started up again with Nick. Though I have climbed 4000 Footers going straight up has always challenged me.

We were slooowly making our way up to Nevada Falls where the crowds had now thinned out, and honestly I would not have wanted to go back down the stony steps. They were slick going up, my falling episodes tend to almost always happen on the way down. It wasn't too long before the husband caught back up with us. His wife decided to just stay at Vernal Falls and the husband continued the mighty climb with us.

After a considerable effort we arrived at the top of Nevada Falls. It was breathtaking. What I couldn't believe was how many people were so close to the edge of the falls itself and even some folks were in the pools at the top, just a slip away from going over the edge. It was then that Nick did tell us of some terrible tales where people have indeed gone over and how quickly it happened.

The husband went back down the way we came. Yes, we did have to go down, but the John Muir Path was much more gradual with plenty of switchbacks and dry. I did feel bad for Nick because we didn't finish until well past 6 pm.

I swear John Muir's spirit was with us on the trip down.

Special thanks to the Mountaineering School in Yosemite! All of the guides were wonderful and super flexible.

I think writing about my Yosemite experience has been both the easiest and most difficult part of this endeavor. Because of it's sheer magnificence and raw beauty there have been so many feelings that flood my being I find no words created by mere mortals worthy enough to describe the full experience. What I really want to do is express that I wish everyone find the thing that fills them with true wonder and have the chance to fully experience that for yourself. My hope is that you don't let fear stop you from having your own experiences.

People are often amazed, bewildered, and shocked that I didn't take this trip with anyone. Now that I reflect on my experience, I can't imagine doing it any other way. To allow myself the freedom to fully feel every emotion without question or judgement, and even selfishly to not have had to share it especially when it was so raw. Yet, I do want to share it with everyone. But rather, wish everyone could experience that feeling for themselves.

WILDWOMEN SUMMIT
THE WILDCATS

Upon returning from Yosemite I joined another Hiking Buddies hike hosted by Nancy. She was on a mission to finish hiking the 48 – 4000 Footers over 70 (48 over 70). She wanted to get possibly the coolest patch out there. It has a hiker with a walker going up the side of a mountain. Thankfully, completing these would also help add to my 48 list.

There ended up being five of us all together. I had posted the Owl's Head write-up on the Hiking Buddies page and didn't realize that it had been well received by some folks. One of those people happened to be joining us on our excursion. With a greeting of "I have been wanting to hike with you since you posted about your Owl's Head Adventure. I loved your write-up and am still laughing about it."

With a greeting like that I knew we were going to have a great day. The five of us started up my very favorite trail in the Whites, the Nineteen Mile Brook Trail. The gradual climb, soft footing and beautiful escort by the Nineteen Mile Brook along side the trail happily babbles to you like an old friend. The brook loves telling you all that's happened since you last met. Nancy, Michele (my first Facebook fan and new friend), Christine, and Dominique moved right along up to the Carter Notch Hut. The trip to the hut added maybe a half mile to the overall trip with a steep in and out but it was time and effort well spent. We got to snack and take time to get to know each other.

My Facebook post write-up was (mostly) as follows:

Four Wildcat Summits with Four Fabulous Wildwomen for the win!

Even though we summitted four peaks only two really counted if you're playing the 4000 Footer Game. We had a total time of 11 hours, 23 minutes, 43 seconds over 8.5 miles. Brought my total count to 14 of the 48 - 4000 Footers.

Not all of the photos are mine. All of the views, stories and laughter were a shared effort. Don't tell my legs that only two of the four mountains were summited counted though. Or my shoulders, or my back, or my arms, or my... pretty sure you get the idea.

I couldn't have done this without the help and inspiration from each one of my hiking mates. One old one (as in having previously hiked with), Nancy Hall, who brought us all together and always impresses me with all she's done and now working on her old geezer patch (her words, not mine, but what a cool patch for 70 and older). New hiking buddies Christine, Dominique, and Michele, who I also consider friends. Once you've shared some good butt sliding (glad I didn't have to worry about packing the snow this time), crawling under fallen trees that threaten to impale you, female anatomy talk (much more informative, and more interesting than TED talks), best peeing methods, and general laugh till you pee antics, you most certainly are considered a friend. And as always, there was interesting conversations. Who knew that people had such passionate feelings about "the flat sheet" or "top sheet"? I just assumed everyone used their sheets the same.

I'm a slow hiker, and when I say slow, well we all decided that there should be a new "speed" named Abbie's pace. Since a lot of groups will list turtles pace, which is typically considered slow (~1 mph) and even those I'm always the slowest. So, the ladies let me lead, and let's just say, no one was left behind.

After going up with a detour down to the Carter Notch Hut, back up and down, and up and down, and up and down and down and down and down and down some more, and up, we realized we had done it. Four consecutive peaks in a row bagged! As we crested the final peak bring us atop Wildcat D, the view took our breath away and the hillside was brimming with wildflowers. We broke out in song with "The Hills are Alive…" followed by "Do-Ra-Me."

I think there may have been some twirling. It is funny how quickly the euphoria can evaporate. After a while, the never ending down and around through the ski slope took its toll. Then the game began of hoping that the each bend would be the last one until finally a shout out for joy that the parking lot was in sight.

I think that physically, this was my most challenging (yes, I probably think this after EVERY hike), though not the longest. Perhaps making it the most rewarding. Though I still haven't learned my lesson on trying to drive 4 1/2 hours home after a day in the Whites. Maybe I'll remember that next time?!?

I had a cutoff time of 6:00 pm for head home time. The plan was to find a place to stay overnight if we finished after that time. We finished around 6:30 and I didn't follow through with the plan to find a place to stay overnight and started driving instead. Only about an hour or so in, I was feeling tired. Because I was coming down Route 16 instead of Route 93, I wasn't going to be stopping at the

Hookset Rest area, always my go to spot about half way and I could have stopped to rest and eat. I didn't have a good route or normal rest spot the way I was going. I would pull off the main road and try to find a safe place to rest. Inevitably all the places would weird me out, so off and on the highway, taking more time, leaving me more tired. Finally, only a little over a half hour from home, was at an actual rest area and slept for an hour or so. Bringing me home about 2:00 am when all was said and done.

Perhaps it was time to start looking at becoming a New Hampshire transplant for real.

LONGEST DAY HIKE
FOR ALZIEMERS

The Hiking Buddies group decided to team up with the Alzheimer's Longest Day Event. To commemorate having just reached 10,000 group members the group's creator, Ben Pease, called out a challenge to The Hiking Buddies. He set a goal of creating 10 Teams with 10 Members each raising $100 resulting in a $10,000 Donation to a great cause.

The evening Ben dropped the challenge on Facebook there were 10 teams created with two of them listed at 1.0 mph (Turtle Pace). I decided to wait to sign up until the next morning and missed out on the turtle paced hikes. Next morning the only "slower" hike listed as 1 – 1.5 for a mountain I hadn't bagged yet was the Osceolas. I went ahead and signed up because I knew I couldn't do anything faster. Because all the teams filled so quickly there were five or six more added. I knew that Nancy had signed up for Hale at a turtles pace and I should have listened to my Jiminy Cricket voice telling me to switch teams.

The Osceolas it would be. I set out to do my fundraising. I met and exceeded my goal of $100 and raised $300. Hiking Buddies ended up having enough Teams to Summit all 48 mountains for the Longest Day Event. The Hiking Buddies came through in flying colors and raised over $50,000 overall! Nice Job Hiking Buddies! Proud to be part of this awesome community.

Not all of the hikes can be favorites. Though I was proud to have participated in the event I knew from the start that there would be some challenges for me. The pace was only one of the things that concerned me. From the beginning I realized that sometimes personalities need to be set aside and I'm still learning how to do that.

Ben had sent a message on the FB page saying that all confirmations would be sent via email. After a day and a half of not seeing a confirmation I started to get nervous because I really wanted to be part of the Longest Day. I reached out to the Team Lead. And thought going to the Team Lead would be the person to ask, knowing that Ben was organizing the Teams and working with the Team Leads. My Team Lead just stated she didn't know if I was on the team, only Ben Pease did. She would find out once the team was filled. Not sure why but it stuck in my craw that the Team Lead didn't seem to want to help by going to Ben.

I went back through my emails one more time and found my confirmation in my junk file. I informed Ben and he posted that people might find their confirmations in their junk folders. I felt like I actually did something that helped the group.

I did the signup online for the fundraising portion of the event through the Alzheimer Foundation. Forgot to sign up on the team Facebook page until only a couple weeks before the event. That's when one of the members asked about peoples pace. Though some said they were turtles, it was clear that the majority of the group was going to be on the 1.5 mph pace.

The hike and pace was pretty much what I expected. I was slow, and ended up being the only one that didn't do the chimney. The chimney is a steep and challenging section but there is a bypass. I listened to the suggestion for taking the bypass down. Since we had to go out and back that way to tag the second peak. The bypass is by no means easy either. For me it was terrifying since you skirt around the edge of a cliff and can't see where you are going. You can, however, see that the drop-off goes for a long way before there is a bottom. I started shaking at one point when all I saw was a drop off and couldn't see where to step down. Thankfully someone was talking me through where to put my foot and once I found the step was good to go.

I was talked into taking the bypass back up. The chimney is nestled in between two rock faces and though the steps are pretty far apart I'm very sure I could have done it. But peer pressure is a funny thing. Knowing that I was already holding the group back, I ended up conceding to the suggestion that I go back on the bypass. I was disappointed in myself for not giving it a go and will return one day to play on the rocks.

The rest of the group was kind of champing at the bit and of course I was fine with letting them go ahead. Actually, I was relieved. Grateful that I did get to chalk up another couple mountain summits on my list.

I really wish the Team Lead didn't feel it necessary to stay with me. Super thankful that another Hiking Buddy did as well. He helped direct some of the questioning and helped with conversation. I tend to not usually do a lot of talking while hiking, the opposite of the Team Lead so the other Buddy was a blessing. I ended up going at an even slower pace in the end than normal.

Afterwards went to the gathering and got to visit with Nancy for a while.

HOSTED FIRST HIKING BUDDIES HIKE

It was finally time for me to host my very own Hiking Buddies Hike. I looked at my list, played with my maps and guidebooks, then decided on Waumbek. That way I could get both a 4000 Footer and 52WAV (Starr King) checked off my list.

I created an event on the Hiking Buddies FB Group. It was titled Tortoise Tuesday #1.

The event had picture of a tortoise and details were as follows:

Slow as we go. There will be huffing, puffing, wheezing and panting... Happy to stop along the way for photos, snacks, drinks, well, and just catch our breath...
This is weather dependent.
Coming up from Connecticut on the 27th, if anyone wants to carpool...

I took my lead from Nancy and set up a group messenger chat for communicating with those that were planning on going. There ended up being seven of us. We started as strangers and left as friends.

My Facebook post hike write-up was as follows:

After years of stalking the Hiking Buddies page, joining a couple of "others" hosting, it was time to throw something out there and see what happens. Awesomeness, that's what happens! Seven strangers brought together by the love of the White Mountains, a common goal of tackling the "48" among other lists. All happy to trudge the path of rocks, roots, moss, natural (man-made) springs, wells, stand-alone fireplaces, and admired views where we could get them at a pace faster than expected.

We started with six official buddies from the parking lot and a random buddy that we were happy to have join us. We did lose our random tag along at our first "ooo" object. A well placed well, about a mile up, OK, a quarter of a mile up. It was more fun thinking that it was a mile and that we were really trail blazing. It was dubbed a mosquito breeding well after all and we decided that perhaps going inside the well for a photo op, was not the best plan. We did get pictures from the outside, and the journey had begun.

The next site to see was the "natural" spring, that appeared to have been created not so naturally. Which provided our first water crossing. Yes, you did have to pay attention, not the usual worrying about where you stepped, but rather to ensure you didn't miss the stream (aka water) you were actually crossing.

At some point we played "guess how old xxx is."

Note to self: "never play that game again…"

We were about a mile in when another of the official Buddie's buddy joined us and we were seven once more. Some of us were Very

Excited about doing natural things in nature (hint, it has to do with what happens when you're well hydrated.) And we were All excited that everyone was indeed well hydrated.

It was a beautiful trail with an amazing group of hiking buddies! True to expectations, there was huffing, puffing, wheezing and panting. We stopped for photos, snacks, drinks, to catch our breath, and go on bio breaks.

I am honored and proud to have new friends thanks to this amazing group. I look forward to more Tortoise hikes in the future.

P.S. Eric Todd Sweet – summit headstand (assistance was required) in your honor…

Post Facebook post information – Eric Todd Sweet is somewhat of a White Mountain legend. He can often be seen on the summit of a 4000 Footer doing his infamous head stand. He's known to many as Candy Man since he posts short videos of himself and his chosen candy of the day. He is a beloved character and loved by many. He is ridiculed by a few, those who I'm sure are jealous of the Candy Man.

TORTOISE TUESDAY #2 ON WEDNESDAY

A month later it was time to schedule another Tortoise Tuesday hike. The reason I chose a Tortoise instead of the typical turtle for my mascot is because I can relate to the Tortoise. They are large, old, and take considerable effort just to get up on their feet. Some days my pack looks and feels like one of their monstrous shells that weigh them down but are very necessary. Plus tortoises do love to eat and I find that to be one of the greatest pleasures of life!

Another two-fer was put in the books. This time Cabot a 4000 Footer and The Horn a 52WAV. Jenn had been on the last hike and was coming up from Rhode Island, so we decided to drive up together and stay in Gorham, New Hampshire. Though we were originally scheduled on a Tuesday, true to my word, I watched the weather and re-scheduled due to an adverse forecast. This caused our Tortoise Tuesday to be on Wednesday.

When I created the event this time I tried to add more detail and it went something like this:

It's just another Tortoise Tuesday. Back by popular demand, a 4000 Footer attempt for those of us who can sometimes make 1 mph pace.

As always this will be slow as we go. There will be huffing, puffing, wheezing and panting... Happy to stop along the way for photos, snacks, drinks, well, and just catch our breath...

This is weather dependent.

Please be prepared with your 10 essentials.

We will be taking the East Approach from York Pond Road. Route will be York Pond Trail, Bunnell Notch Trail, Kilkenny Ridge/Mt. Cabot Trail. Out and back is 9.6 mi with 2900 ft elev gain.

Once we hit Cabot if we're going at breakneck speed and feeling ambitious, we can do the loop to tag The Bulge and The Horn via Unknown Pond Trail. Doing the loop is 11.6 mi with 3300 ft elev gain. What's an extra two miles with some short ledge scrambles followed by a difficult scramble?

My post hike write-up went something like this...

Another Epic Hiking Buddies Hike. A couple days late and more than a couple dollars short comes the trip report for Tortoise Tuesday (on Wednesday.) The Tortoise crew triumphed for a completion of Cabot and a bonus extra couple of bumps thrown in, The Bulge (let's not get personal), and The Horn with a finish by Unknown Pond (but now that it is known, can't we give it a better name?)

Thanks to the all the buddies for coming out and up to the most Northern of the 4000 Footers. There were six of us that started and one joined us before we hit the first peak.

Did you all know that a group of tortoises is called a creep which seems fitting for us, not for the reason that may have just crossed your mind. The creep did creep along and we did keep to creep pace up to the summit of Cabot. But before we could summit I led us on many miles of bug eating, spider web wrapping and overgrowth scraping. At one point I came upon a poor garter snake where we both simultaneously got startled. Squiggles (of course I named it) actually jumped up and ran away after I did my girliest scream and jumped myself. Have you seen a snake run, well running without legs is well, kind of impossible, so Squiggles looked like a bunch of its namesake, and in a flurry scurried into the underbrush. Poor thing…

Being in the lead it didn't take long for me to feel like Frodo in Shelob's lair since I was wrapped up in spider web material from head to foot. I figure if all the spiders talked to each other they might have made a tasty meal of me. Luckily others on Team Tortoise were also gluttons for punishment and I was grateful for others to lead us forward.

Always interesting conversations to listen in on, well, I'd say participate in, but I'm usually just trying not to trip and continue to breathe. I have found that breathing is important not just in getting to one's destination but in general. I do love learning new things and it seems that air fryers are pretty awesome, which I would have never known otherwise.

Where else can lawyers, engineers, health care providers, educators, accountants, entrepreneurs, retirees of all sorts, writers, realtors, service industry workers, and basically any type of employment and background come together and walk for hours, talking, or not and feel a connection larger than themselves? Sharing stories of summits completed, attempted or planned for the future with all the same enthusiasm of waiting to see what Santa brought you on Christmas morning?

The journey of the 48 starts with a single step onto the majestic Whites and this special group has brought so many together so that we don't have to do it alone. I for one am someone that has enjoyed much solitude in the midst of the company of Hiking Buddies as well. If you are someone who has been watching in the wings, I strongly recommend joining an event, and even if you join one that didn't work for you, don't give up, there are Buddies for everyone, give another group a try. Or host an event of your own. I digress...

We reached the underwhelming views of Mount Cabot and a cairn that was also underwhelming. Yet, oh so satisfying to say that we made it. But first we had a rest at the Cabot Cabin, quaint, and there was a toilet, though reserved for solids. Pretty sure it has been used for relieving oneself of liquids as well, since a toilet in the woods is a luxury or not, I did not step inside, but the view I had was much nicer than the wooden door in a hot, smelly, and probably spidery box...

We did not linger long at the Cabot summit since we snacked earlier and had other stuff to experience. Next, we summitted The Bulge, well, we did it because it was on the path and rather unavoidable. I'd say it was more a blip than a bulge, but what do I know?

Onto The Horn, a 52WAV. At this time, I was bringing up the rear at this point as Dominique and I approached, the other five of the creep were atop the rock slab of the summit. And though I wouldn't say I have a fear of heights, I certainly have a respect for gravity. At first followed Dominique up a tall narrow strip of rock that had a couple foot crevasse to the summit slab. Then of course I looked to my left and saw the forty-foot drop and decided to try to find another way up. So, I wound my way around to where the others had gone. And I did try, but actual climbing up a line to the slab was not to be my way. Back to the beginning, and up the narrow ledge that I gave up earlier and though still freaked out by the 40-

foot drop, then focused on Dominique's wise words, "just don't look that way."

With my heart beating in my ears, I did as I was instructed and defying gravity, we were a creep once more. Of course, from the top, it was "easy" to see a favorable descent. After snacking, sunbathing, picture taking, admiring views and the conversion of some to the ways of the summit ibuprofen ritual, the creep continued.

We reached the next point of interest, which I like to call "The Mosquito Maker."

While pictures were taken by some, I stole off for my 76th pee pit. At least I knew I was keeping hydrated. Some mud slogging, scaring many a frog, and plenty of greenery we came to the end of our journey.

Thank you all for making it another memorable hike and new friendships forged! Happy trails from the tortiest of tortoises…

After staying overnight once more Jenn and I decided to hit Mount Hale on the way out of Dodge.

Hale Yeah!

Number 19 of 48 on the books. Thanks to Jenn for being my partner in crime. The day after another Tortoise takeover.

Before, during and after pics were posted to show the good, the hot, and the sweaty. At least they weren't scratch and sniff…

And who says there's no views from Hale? You just have to know where to look.

This may have been the shortest hike to the summit so far, but to quote my hiking buddy "it was no joke."

Luckily the trail was as mystical and magical as those that have come before. I'm still waiting to see some fairies amongst the ferns and the mushrooms.

NANCY IS A BADASS

The accomplishment that is my favorite to boast about isn't even mine, it's Nancy's. She was one summit away from earning for her "Old Geezer" patch. She just had one more 4000 Footer to check off her list. It just happened to be the second highest mountain in New England.

Nancy is the least Geezerie over 70s person I know! She is one of my favorite people that I've met through Hiking Buddies NH48 and a total badass. I'm grateful that she's so willing to share her experience with anyone,especially me. Plus, her fortitude and patience is endless.

I think it was fitting that one of the greatest women I have the pleasure of knowing asked if I wanted to accompany her on her quest to summit one of the greatest mountains in The Whites. The plan was try and tag on Mount Madison, since I still needed Madison. We planned an overnight stay on the Madison Hut.

Post hike post was put on FB as follows…

CONGRATULATIONS to Nancy Hall!!!!!

48 over 70 complete – or as Nancy likes to say that she's earned her Old Geezer Patch.

We were planning to have a threesome, for the hike, with another one of our favorite hiking buddies. As the time came closer and we were watching the weather forecast, sometimes hourly as one does, especially if attempting a Northern Presi. The third person of our potential party indicated concern and rightly so, with potential T-storms possible. Well, though I also had some reservations, sometimes I'm also skeptical about the details of a forecast, and Nancy said she was going for it, so go for it we did.

We stayed at the Art Gallery Hostel in Whitefield, NH. My first hostel experience. I would recommend it, though I did have to wrestle my food bag away from the resident feline. Apparently she had a hankering for beef jerky (cats…) A pit stop for caffeine and we were off to the trailhead.

There were several trails that can take you to the Hut. The most popular and direct route is the Airline Trail. This is where Nancy's experience was called into play. She told of a story of getting caught on the Airline Trail when the weather turned on her and with the trail being exposed she used the cutoff path to get over to the Valley Way Trail which is not exposed. The Valley Way Trail is in the woods offering protection from severe elements until you are pretty much at the hut. With the weather forecast showing potential Thunderstorms on our way up we decided to stick to the walk in the woods trail. Being a confirmed tree hugger, that was the perfect choice for me.

The forecast had actually improved some as we were on trail and T-storms weren't expected until late afternoon. We started our hike about a half hour earlier than planned. As we started heading up, there were streaks of light making their way through the trees. The sun stayed out and the heat increased, this was not the forecast. But the company was great and I do enjoy hearing Nancy's stories. She is always well prepared and one is in good hands with her on your side.

The first couple miles seemed to move quickly. I started getting hangry and needed snacks, so Nancy obliged. Then the "just keep moving" upwards kicked in. We arrived at the Madison Hut, dropped the non-essentials, ate some more food, looked up at the pile of rocks and off we went. It was "only" about a mile to the summit, but it was no easy task to get there. I did my best to keep up, but Nancy just picked her way through the relentless rock pile, and we agreed that we'd take it one cairn at a time. About a quarter of the way there the rain clouds rolled in and quite literally out of nowhere. Nancy asked if I was still going because she was. A little or even a lot of rain was not a deterrent. Nancy led and, in awe, I did my best to follow. At first the rain was welcoming, then it just unleashed the water, and THAT's when we decided to put on rain gear, and almost as soon as we put our rain gear on then packs back on, it was over. The mountain top was steaming and so were we. We shed our sweltering suits and continued to pick our way up, one steamy boulder at a time.

Ta da… We made it! Nancy finished another 48-4000 Footer accomplishment! 48 over 70. Actually, it wasn't complete until we were back down, but I took a picture with her holding the Finisher sign atop Adams anyways. Even though the patch has a hiker with a walker and Nancy will wear hers with pride, I think I'm the one that will need the walker.

From the hut we had taken the Airline Trail to Adams. This is the most direct route but arguably the toughest. We tried to take the Gulfside Trail down, which is a more gentle grade and much more walkable but ended back up on Airline Trail. At one point we noticed a herd path amongst the thick blanket of blueberry bushes that looked like it connected to the Gulfside Trail. The Gulfside Trail didn't look very far away and as far as we could tell the herd path would take us there. We started on the bushwack and the herd path disappeared. Nancy was a bit ahead of me and said she'd go first and when she got to the actual trail stated "I don't think that's a good way."

The other option was to skirt across the top of a rather large basin. This basin was lined with loose rocks all the way on to the top. The bottom of the basin was about 40 ft below, well, at least that's where the loose rock wall ended. Not sure what was on the bottom because there was a blanket of shrubbery below. So, I stepped from the blueberry covering onto the top of the crater, and had about 60 feet along this edge that I needed to traverse. Each step I took was precarious and I felt the whole wall beneath me shift on each step. I held my breath and just kept moving until I was a couple feet from where Nancy was and stepped swiftly off the edge of doom. We both agreed that neither way was ideal, but my way wasn't probably a very smart way to go after all. Hind sight is always 20/20.

We did make it back to the hut JUST in time for dinner.

If you see this awesome lady on your journey, make sure you say hello and if you ever need help while you're out on the trail, she is always more than happy to help.

CONGRATULATIONS!!!!!!!!!!!! Can't say it enough!

You're my Hero! Thanks for sharing your journey with me!

We had planned on hiking up Madison the next morning. From the hut it's Just Right There. With less than a half mile to the summit it would be a quick trip in the morning.

I love staying at the huts. Another controversial issue for many in the hiking community. Some folks would have all the huts torn down and let the mountains go back to all natural. Others, like myself, enjoy having a little piece of comfort, community, and history lessons that the AMC provides through this service. The croo always does a great job and this visit they put on a little safety skit. It was entertaining and informative. Nancy and I probably should have seen it before doing our little bushwack earlier.

The other thing I enjoy is the cross section of those that take advantage of the hut's services. That night we sat with a gentleman, probably my age, going hut to hut, a family with kids ranging from elementary age to one heading off to college soon. Nancy talked to the young woman who was college bound about horses. I watched the younger boys play board games after dinner. Then we all turned in.

I chose a bunk above Nancy against the windows. The winds picked up. It was amazing to watch as if a hurricane blew all around us but the hut was solid and though it sounded like a freight train gong by we couldn't feel a thing. Whether you believe in the great beyond. I swear I saw Kate Matrosova (if you don't know who she is I encourage you to read Ty Gagne's book 'Where You'll Find Me') blow by my window as she searched for somewhere to come in out of the cold.

The next morning the croo woke us with a song. For the life of me can't remember what it was. They set their own words to some recognizable tune. It was a much more fun way to be woken up than an alarm assaulting you to start your day. With a not so great forecast many were persuaded to not do summit hikes.

With the wind definitely much subsided from the night before I decided that I wanted to go ahead and give Madison a try. We packed up just our essentials and would get our overnight gear after summiting, since we'd have to go past the hut on our way back.

We walked towards the path but the fog was thick and oh so eerie. Everything was wet and even though the wind had settled a lot it wasn't completely gone.

We started up the rocky scramble and I began to slip right out of the gate. Then the hair stood up on the back of my neck. The vision of Kate from the night before flashed across my mind. I just looked at Nancy and said "I'm not feeling it."

So, we headed back to the hut. Finished packing. Most everyone was gone, just a couple of folks heading out, a couple of croo, and an AT thru hiker. Paying his service for a stay overnight. That's another service that I like from the AMC hut system, they will provide food and if they have space a place to sleep on return for work from AT thru hikers.

Keep up the good work AMC. I support you.

SOMETIMES THE BEST DAYS
DON'T GO AS PLANNED

Would this be the time to finally get Isolation? I was hoping to knock off another peak from my list of "Don't Finish On" peaks. Stacy had set up a Hiking Buddies event for Isolation. We'd go up Glen Boulder Trail onto Isolation and out Rocky Branch. Rocky Branch is notoriously long, swampy and buggy. So, I was kind of looking forward to tackling this with friends in addition to scratching it off my list.

Mount Isolation attempt was not to be instead we did land Mount Parker (a 52 WAV) for the win. The rest of this chapter is dedicated to the rest of the story.

As always, a hiking adventure in the White Mountains begins with a verrrry long and tedious drive (at least for me at that time). After four and a half hours on the road I made it to another hostel. I never really thought I'd be a hostel person, no not hostile because I can sometimes be that, but the thought of sharing a room with a half dozen other people or so isn't fitting with my agoraphobia. Most people I know who'd backpacked through Europe talked about staying in hostels, and conditions didn't sound so inviting. I must say, I was pleasantly surprised at how welcoming The Notch Hostel was. It actually reminded me of growing up and sharing a room with my sisters, so it kind of felt at home. And how fitting since I was meeting up with one of my hiking buddies who feels like a sister when we share our adventures on the trail.

While waiting for this hiking sister, hister, siker, sounded better in my head. Instead, we'll just call her Michele, well, since that's her name. I took the time to scope where to have dinner before Michele arrived. It's one of the many reasons I used to run and now hike, because I really love to eat. Well, "Cheese Louise" was closed, yes, I was sold based on the name, because one of my weaknesses is cheese. Lactaid is this gal's best friend. I settled for my second runner up was the "Almost There Restaurant". Michele arrived, but since she'd already eaten I took off to check out the eatery.

My five star review: It is definitely a local favorite, which is always a good sign. The fish and chips was possibly the best I have ever eaten and it came so fast I was afraid it would be that heat lamp warm. That turned out to not be the case. The fish was divine and the batter was light and crispy.

OK, not the most eloquent review, but it most definitely was the best fish and chips I've ever had. Sometimes not getting what you want at first can be a blessing. Little did I know that this would be a recurring theme this trip. It was tasty, hot, and there was definitely more fish than batter. I'm hoping to return to check out their other items.

After returning to the hostel, I caught up with my friend and we turned in. There was only one other woman in the room and it turned out that she was going to be on the hike, one of the later starters of course. After a surprisingly good night's sleep I was up early, 4:00 am or so, and we headed out. The plan was a quick stop at Dunkin, how awesome that they opened at 4:30. Well, I had technical difficulties, basically getting my shit together. I used to think I was a morning person, but at 4:30, trying to find my reading glasses and turn on my google maps was enough to have me running circles around my car before leaving the hostel. I went back and forth from seat to trunk and back again. So, after starting early, by the time I got myself together and met up with Michele, well, we were now running on the "hope we can make it in time for our 5:30 start time."

Because this was a traverse, we needed to drop one car at the Rocky Branch Trailhead. We met there and I grabbed my pack and finished gulping down the much-needed caffeine. I hopped into Michele's vehicle (really people, yes, I don't remember what she drives, don't judge…) and off we headed to Glen Ellis Falls parking lot. We met up with the third party from the turtle paced group. There were supposed to be four of us but the fourth was a no show. We were about a half hour behind our getting started time and that's when I realized my poles were back in my car. Knowing it was going to be a VERY long day anyways, I decided to carry on without them. And I am someone who relies heavily on their poles, so perhaps what happened was the way the day was supposed to go. The trail started right away with much up and "scrambling" as they say, so not having the poles actually freed up my hands and as I grabbed ahold of a rock, root or tree I felt the squish and sliminess of some poor slug as I put an untimely end to its brief life… Yup, it was going to be one of those kind of days.

The scramble went quickly and it was nice getting to know a new hiking buddy. We were about three quarters of a mile up and entered the alpine zone. The most magical of all the mountains areas, with the stunted trees, moss, and lichen. I'm always waiting for the fairies to show themselves. When I stepped out of the treeline and stood up,

I felt that feeling. It was the "this is not good" feeling. Michele and I had discussed the wind perhaps being an issue. Weather forecast had 50 to 70 mph gusts early and showed it would be diminishing during the day. It was a little after 6 am and the winds were at least 50 mph steady. That unnerving freight train roar was present and that was enough for me to say "I'm not feeling it."

Michele and I were in agreement and retreated while our new friend decided to go on. She was unperturbed by the winds. On the way down Michele and I crossed paths with the fearless Stacy, who had organized this hike, and was in the slow to moderate group. All the Jen(n)s were with her along with Laurelyn who was finishing her 48th on Isolation. They were also unperturbed (I know when telling a story it's bad form to use the same word multiple times in the same paragraph, but it is such a fitting word) by the blowing of the winds and we wished them a safe hike and hoped to see them all some other time along the White Mountain trails.

We got to the parking lot, and did I mention that there's an actual bathroom there? Yes, it's an outhouse but it has a seat and you only have to hover if you want to. You're welcome ladies.

We decided to run up to the Pinkham Notch welcome center so we could make a new plan since neither of our phones had service. Perhaps a 52 WAV would be best. Because my sense of direction is ass backwards, and of course that meant I was navigating, told Michele to go in the wrong direction out of the parking area. I quickly realized my mistake, well after Google Maps kept telling us to U-turn. We got turned back to the correct direction without having gone too far. And this is why I consider Michele a sister of the White Mountains, because she was unperturbed (yes, I know it's THAT word again) by my lack of an internal compass.

We finally arrived at the visitor center and Oohed and Ahhhed at the really cool 3D display of the White Mountains. Then found the

52 WAV book to determine what was doable. Though Stairs Mountain and Mount Resolution were nearby we settled in on Mount Parker. Off we went to pick up my car and drive to our new destination. We got out of the car and started suiting back up, yeah, I had my poles only to find that we'd been foiled again. As we were getting ready, or maybe even before that, Michele received a message that our third party that had decided to continue on had fallen and gotten hurt. That's not what foiled us, but it did make us concerned for her. I now had my poles, but now Michele did not.

Remember the toilets at the Glen Ellis Falls parking lot, well, that was where Michele's poles were propped. So, off we went, another detour, which I didn't mind, since it was snack time and I always have plenty of snacks.

We arrived as the injured party was getting off the trail, so we got to at least see her, she had seen Michele's poles and was going to send a message. And I got to sit on a toilet once more before we'd be back to dropping drawers, even with my lovely funnel that helps me pee like a man, still have to bare all, as it were. All was right with the world again, and back to the trailhead we went.

Mount Parker is a treasure. We had the trail and summit mostly to ourselves. We got to relax on top and had a great view of the mountain we'd started to summit that morning. We were both grateful that we chose to change course. There was no wind and wonderful views. And we did see some mystical creatures' homes on our way through the woods.

I chose to stay at the hostel that night. Unfortunately my allergies had kicked in. And of course that night the room was full. I turned in really early and was probably asleep by 7:30 pm. I woke around 12:30 am and started with a coughing fit. Having just come out of a global pandemic, and knowing that COVID was alive and well, I decided that coughing was not something a room full of people in their beds would be interested in listening to. Rather than fretting about it and trying to stifle coughs until morning came I got up. I had a few good hours of sleep and most importantly had a hot shower before bed helped me decide to gather my things and hope that that noise was less obnoxious to all than me stifling my coughs would be. I drove the four and a half hours home and crawled back into my own bed for a few more hours of blissful sleep.

ZBONDS TRAVERSE WITH A 48 FINISHER

One of the Wildwomen was trying to finish her 48. She just needed to get The Bonds which included West Bond, Bondcliff and Mount Bond. She was signed up with a hiking buddies group that would have made that happen. But the weather in The Whites can be fickle, so after being rescheduled twice they ended up cancelling the hike. I just made an innocent comment to her that I'd join her if they didn't end up going. Sure enough Christine took me up on my offer. She asked if I'd set up a Hiking Buddies hike so she could FINALLY get the elusive final three for her big finish. I was honored.

Though I'm not gonna lie, as I started planning the hike I said to myself, "Abbie, This is another fine mess that you've gotten us into…"

The Tortoise Takeover of the Bonds Hiking Buddies event was born.

The event details were as follows:

It's time for a Tortoise Takeover of the Bonds. An over-nighter for the creep (group of tortoises that is), who can sometimes make a 1 mph pace.

As always this will be slow as we go. Probably not a group to go with if you really want to see some wildlife as there will be huffing, puffing, wheezing and panting... Happy to stop along the way for photos, snacks, drinks, well, and just catch our breath...

This is weather dependent.

Please be prepared with your 10 essentials and gear for camping out overnight.

We will start this journey at the Lincoln Woods Visitor Center. We'll travel 2.9 miles (but who's counting) on Lincoln Woods Trail, then 6.2 miles on the Bondcliff Trail to summit Bondcliff, continue 1.2 miles to Mt. Bond, then the half mile plus to the Guyot Campsite. Set up camp then head to West Bond on West Bond Spur for sunset (if all goes according to plan). Bring a headlamp with extra batteries in order to return to camp. After a long day on the trail we'll get a good night sleep in the mountain fresh air. Pack up the next morning and out from whence we came. We may have at least one 48 completer on this trip. Won't that be exciting?!?!?

Total round trip will be approx. 23 miles with 4800 ft elevation gain and the satisfaction of having three 4000 Footers under your belt.

I'm tired just writing up the plan... sheesh...

Honestly, I didn't really know if I was up for an actual backpacking trip. As much as I would daydream about being an AT thru-hiker one day, or even a professional section hiker. The thought of carrying everything I need to survive for even a couple of days made my back hurt. Talk about Tortoise Pace, or even Abbie pace, what could be slower than that?

We had a great group assembled. Nancy (the only female in the group with backpacking experience), Dominique (one of the Wild-women), Christine (our potential 48 finisher), Kerri (the woman whom I'd met, briefly hiked with on the Isolation attempt, who had fallen and turned out had fractured her hand after all), Myself, and Franko (our token male) who I'm sure was wondering what in the world he'd gotten himself into.

We watched the weather, changed the date, which was why one of our favorite turtles (Ms. Nancy) was able to join us. I had originally planned on an out and back hike. Nancy suggested we do the traverse and those of us who needed it could get Zealand and most importantly, we'd only need to hike Lincoln Woods once on this trip instead of out and back.

The original plan was to go in and out Lincoln Woods. This route was a copy of the hike that Christine was signed up to do with the Hiking Buddies group that got canceled. Reflecting on the Owl's Head death march, I start to involuntarily shake at the thought of hiking Lincoln woods once, much less twice in as many days. So, when Nancy suggested eliminating one Lincoln Woods and adding another 4000 Footer, well who was I to argue with that? Who am I kidding? I was ecstatic. Yes! I'm in. I checked with Christine, and she was onboard and the route was changed.

In the planning stage Nancy had the foresight to suggested that we consider hiring Redline Guiding to have a porter take our tents up to the campsite and set up since we were now going to be hiking on the weekend. This wasn't going to be any weekend but one of the nicest at the end of the summer. Anyone that knows anything about the White Mountains knows that the end of summer would bring the crowds as well as the AT thru hikers for the AT. We all jumped at the chance and were grateful to not have an extra four-ish pounds to carry for at least that first day. Not to mention that we (or at least I) am slow going and add all of the overnight stuff to the standard 10 essentials, plus all of the items that "might" be needed if something were to go awry, any little help was welcome. Perhaps I should stop reading about all of the catastrophes that have befallen those that have needed SAR to come to their aid and I might be able to shed a pound or three from my pack. After all with three nurses, a respiratory therapist, retired engineer, and someone with military experience, we most certainly had the skillset to face any situation.

The start time got earlier and earlier as we fine-tuned plans until we agreed that those of us leaving our vehicles at the Lincoln Woods Visitor Center would get picked up by Nancy at 4:30 in order to meet up with Dominic (our porter) not to be confused with the very awesome Dominique who was one of our group members. He was to meet us at Zealand Trailhead and we would give him our tents to set up at the Guyot Campsite.

Saturday morning a little after 4 am, I pulled into a fairly full parking lot where one of our Buddies was already there, so I pulled in next to her. Shortly after I parked Dominique arrived. I started doing my "getting myself and my shit together" routine. Not wanting to forget anything took me even longer than the week before, because I certainly did not want to be without poles on this hike. Back and forth, around and back again, open the pack, check for water, maps, keys, hiking shoes on, ok, one more check, just one more, OK, almost ready. Meanwhile, Dominique and our other Buddy were asking about what kind of car Nancy drives, to which I'm useless, shrug my shoulders, and check stuff just ONE more time.

Expecting Nancy to just swing in to pick us up we were surprised she wasn't there. Our Buddy called out and we were able to find her, a few changeout of items from her car so we had room, and a quest for her missing jet boil lid. We were on our way.

We made it to the Zealand Trailhead where we met Christine (our Hiker of Honor) and Dominic was waiting to take our tents.

After snapping a few pictures we were on our way to an epic two-day adventure. The ladies all felt like tortoises as we ended up carrying everything but the kitchen sink. Welllll, maybe you could say that we did carry the kitchen sink as there were a couple of jet boils, pretty sure each of us had a water filtration system, and enough food to feed not only an army but also all the thru hikers on the AT. However, that did not stop some of us from enjoying a piece of cake at the Zealand Hut.

Shoutout to Redline Guiding for helping us ensure we had a place to lay our heads at the Guyot Campsite! I'm sure that Dominic (our porter, not to be confused with our very own Dominique) appreciated not having to escort us until we had gotten to the campsite. With the extra weight I'm pretty sure we moved at an even slower than Abbie pace. Which is normally between a turtle's pace and sloth pace, but still faster than a snail's pace.

We traversed from the Zealand trail, with a pit stop at the Zealand Hut. This led us into a false sense of hiking security, since it was probably the easiest couple of miles I've actually hiked in the Whites. Except that last couple hundred feet to get UP to the Hut. It was still nice to drop the packs for a bit and use the facilities. Was hoping to caffeinate up, but the croo was doing a changeover and there was no extra coffee boost. I just had to rely on the piece of cake to do the job. There were some nice views from the hut though and we hoisted the packs back on and on to the next point of interest.

We also got to hear about the hiker who stripped, climbed on the top of the hut and yelled incoherent threats. Seems we missed the entertainment by a couple of days. We all wondered where he kept the weapon since he was dressed in his birthday suit.

I'd read in the White Mountain Guidebook that the views from Zeacliff were some of the best in the White Mountains, so of course those of us that went to see the incredible views, got to see the clouds roll in and then we were in the middle of the clouds, so I can not confirm or deny what has been written. It did have an eerie feeling and we were waiting for the off key music, wondering if we'd accidentally entered into a 1950s horror movie. Of course when, we got back to the main trail and all was clear again.

Almost as soon as we were back on the trail we ran into Dominic. He'd already been to the campsite and gotten us set up. We all liked how he stated that he, "expected to see us 'closer' to the Zealand summit."

Translation "OMG, you guys move sooooo slow."

Afterwards we thought about giving him more stuff to take up. Another missed opportunity.

We sauntered along and made it to the Zealand turn off soon enough and some of us went to the summit without a view. We met some cool pups (no I'm not making fun of young people, there were some nice puppy dogs.) I do think Zealand has the coolest summit sign though.

I grumbled and maybe even cried a little at having to put the pack back on, and needed assistance to do so. That was when I was told that my pack was so light. It sure didn't feel light to me. And with each mile it got heavier. We were greeted with some wonderful views, and another chance to shed the pack. Some pictures and back at it.

At long last, we arrived at the campsite, we let out a little cheer, then followed the "The Caretaker is Currently è" sign. Dominic had informed us that we were set up on Platforms 9 & 10. We went DOWN, past Platforms 1 & 2, DOWN, past Platforms 3 & 4, DOWN, past Platforms 5 & 6, DOWN, no signs of our tents or the caretaker. At long last we see the caretaker, Andrew, on Platform 7 or 8, with a few gathered around. He welcomed us and gave us the low down, dos and don'ts. Then pointed DOWN, to where we were set up, yes, the end of the line as it were. There were 4 tents on Platform 9. Yes, you guessed it, DOWN some more was my tent all on its own on Platform 10.

The four other women ended up together. Franko had his tent with him and set up on the platform with me. The walk down to the tents all but did me in. Though I was disheartened about being set up on the platform furthest down, the silver lining was that we were close to the privy.

Nancy and Franko stayed at camp while the rest of us decided to head to West Bond. Originally, we planned to go for sunset but made a better decision to go in daylight. The rest of us lightened our loads and had something to eat. We headed out and were amazed how quickly we were able to skip up to West Bond. Now THAT was a spectacular view. We were not disappointed. And we got to enjoy the summit to ourselves for a short while. As we were headed back to camp, it seemed everyone at camp was heading to West Bond for sunset.

Honestly, I would not have enjoyed the sunset because I would have worried the whole time about the rock scramble coming off of West Bond in the dark. Nor would I have enjoyed being up on the summit with so many people. It was nice to get back, eat our dinner, and turn in early. We planned to be up and out early the next morning.

One of the most important things to do when camping in the back country is to utilize the bear boxes. There was one provided by the AMC at the campsite. I brought everything over and stowed away my food before we went to West Bond, well except for the small baggie of trail mix in the side pocket of my pack. Which only crossed my mind about 2 am, after a brief out of the tent for my middle of the night bladder relief outing. I crawled back into my tent and snuggled up in my sleeping bag, ahh ready to drop back off to slumberland, then…

The platform jiggled, and I could hear something being "dragged" across the platform. I stopped breathing, listened, then heard the low guttural growling that I could only imagine was a bear sniffing out a snack.

With my heart pounding and waiting for a giant paw coming through to shred my tent. It was at this moment that I remembered that two ounces of trail mix was still in my pack. And of course my pack was being used as my pillow. I hear the shuffle a couple more times and continued to listen to the "grunting" only to realize it's my platform partner snoring. And the dragging sound was when he would shift, rubbing his tent bottom along the platform. Relief washed over me an it is at these times that I find my overactive imagination a nuisance...

Morning came and I was in one piece. Up early so I could get to the privy before the masses. I got a picture from my platform of the light before sunrise. But the best view was from the path to the privy, so that is where I got to see the sunrise and leave a little compostable material as a thank you.

We were all trying to find ways to lighten our loads, since now we really were like the turtle carrying our homes on our backs as well. So, my extra canister for the jet boil along with several food packets from Christine and odd items from others were donated to the caretaker. Andrew didn't realize he was going shopping when he took a stroll in the morning to see how we were making out. If he was only a woman, size 8, he would have been the recipient of all my extra clothes as well.

A hot cup of coffee and off we went. Thankful for the platform that helped me put on my pack. A little cursing at why the hell I brought so many extra clothes and trying to eat as much food as possible got me probably to the same weight I'd had the day before. A little teetering until stability kicked in and UP and out we went.

It seemed like it took no time at all to get to Mount Bond. And from there we could see the Ridge to Bondcliff. We had the most spectacular views for our morning greeting. I think for the very first time I actually felt like a hiker. I was even able to get a few feet ahead of the group to take pictures of those behind me. It was a stunning walk along the ridge and Bondcliff was all that I imagined. It was an "I can't believe I did it" moment as I crawled out to the cliff for what we called "the money shot".

We celebrated Christine's accomplishment. How excited we all were for her. We were on a high as we started our way down and out. Glad that I'd read, ahead of time, about where there was one challenging section that it was suggested we pass down our packs. Thanks to Feliciano for being our pack catcher.

Then it was the loooooong walk out. Yes, it was flat, but man was it long. Still, Lincoln Woods will never be as long as it was the day (and night) we did Owls Head. I had not much love for it this time around either.

That was definitely my most challenging AND Rewarding hike up to that date! To quote, or more likely misquote Nancy, "there's something extremely satisfying in doing difficult things."

That made it official and I was half way there (24/48)!

Couldn't have done it without my Hiking Buddies!

A 4000 FOOTER JUNIOR

Officially more than halfway now and one of my hiking buddies told me that I was a Junior. To which I responded by cocking my head like a cocker spaniel and blinking, non-comprehendingly. He went on to explain that with 48 – 4000 Footers they can be broken up into 4 sets of 12. You're a Freshman when working on the first 12. Then you become a Sophomore when you move onto 13 through 24. The lucky ones like me move onto a Junior when you hit 25 through 36. Yes, then Senior for the final stretch.

Then I replied, "that's brilliant!"

OK, maybe I didn't say that, but it IS brilliant!

I couldn't believe that the ZBONDs Traverse was three months earlier. Thankfully my people don't care how unfit I am and still join me in my quest. Nancy had been reaching out and almost got me back out on the trail earlier. I had missed hiking with her, so was happy that she was willing to join me for something to get me moving again.

Why has it been so long? Well, after the incredible ZBONDs adventure things got busy, as they do. COVID finally found me, so that was a couple weeks of not funness. Then it was time to start looking for a new residence, since my situation was only temporary after selling my house. So, hiking was put on hold as I went in search of a new abode. My ultimate goal was to move closer to the love of my life, that would be the White Mountains which I think I fall in love with a little more each time I experience their splendor. Rather than do another temporary move in Connecticut, which I had contemplated, because I still have my Connecticut peeps that I enjoy hanging out with. I decided to make the leap and head to New Hampshire. It only took a couple of home hunting trips and the perfect place. I did put an offer on one not-so-perfect place, but that's another story, and thankfully it fell through.

After closing on the most perfect of places, moving some stuff in, taking three days to get internet service, and much frustration at trying to activate all of my "SMART" home devices it was time for a hike break. Though, without a doubt, this hike was more sobering knowing that the missing hiker had not been found after several days of being missing.

It was time to get the gear ready, winter weather hiking in the Whites takes a bit more thoughtfulness and ensuring that I had all the right stuff. My wool base layer had been turned to swiss cheese since I didn't properly store it and the moths were apparently very hungry this spring and summer. So it was time to try the new one. Find the microspikes – check, extra warm layers – check, bivy (plus extra space blanket) – check, headlamp – check, first aid kit (though going with Nancy, my first aid kit is like child's play, she's got the good stuff), I won't bore you with the rest. Loaded up the pack, made sure fitting is good, charge up Garmin Inreach Mini2, attached to pack and ready for the morning.

Morning comes, a good breakfast, fix some food, make the special choco-coffee for my summit treat. I need motivation and that was supposed to be it. Get to the Highland Center early and Nancy comes early. We gear up, pay for parking, one final pee indoors, back to the car, microspikes and backpacks on, and off we go. Couldn't have asked for a better day to tackle Mount Tom.

There's something magical about walking on a snow covered path in the woods especially when you're in good company. Then of course we come to the first water crossing. It hasn't been cold and snowy enough to create comfortable snow bridges and this "stream" stretches a good 40 yards or so. There was a pretty good path along a fallen tree trunk with some solid ice build up along the trunk to get us across safely. There were a few ice flows to navigate. With me in the lead Nancy got to see where not to go.

We did encounter a few others and I think we all were still hoping for the missing hiker, Emily Sotelo, to be found safe. I felt there was genuine concern for each of us to be safe and that was somehow more prevalent than I've ever felt before.

We moved along pretty smoothly on the Avalon trail, then onto the A-Z trail and there was a little more up to it. I started to slow and stop more often. I called out for a snack break and polished off half my ham sandwich and half my PBJ. I was looking forward to just a swig of my steamy cocktail to help give me a little boost and of course my proverbial carrot to get me to the summit. I reached for my thermos, but there was no thermos. "Nooooooooo…"

I did have plenty of water, but it is the little things that can seemingly make or break a good time. Then, my hero, "I have chocolate to share with you when we get there," and all was right with the world again.

There was more up, and a lot more huffing and puffing, and stopping, and water breaks (in and out). Probably a little cursing but mostly just hurumphing. From time to time we'd stop to take in the views and though there weren't clear vistas, somehow looking through the trees and seeing the mountain views out in the distance is still very mystical.

Another summit reached and a pleasant decent. We did have a good laugh when we came to the junction and a couple that were probably half our age stated "go ahead, you're probably faster than us."

We just laughed…

We got back to the water crossing, well our safe passage ice-bridge has all but collapsed. So we had a very "exciting" crossing on the way back across the "stream". What Nancy called exciting I called terrifying, and though the water wasn't deep, it was just the thought of a misplaced step into a set of rocks that could twist you up in a heartbeat that scared me.

I think we (ok maybe it was just me) skipped the rest of the way to the car.

I said a silent prayer for Emily, "Be safe out there wherever you are."

MISSING YOUNG WOMAN SHAKES THE HIKING COMMUNITY

The day Nancy and I hiked Mount Tom was the day that they found Emily. Emily Sotelo was a bright, beautiful, and kind young woman who went missing the day before her 20th Birthday. It was five days after she went missing that she was found on Mount Lafayette. With high winds and cold temperatures, she lost her way and was off trail but heading down off the summit. She was found about a half mile off the trail where it's suspected that she followed a drainage down to the headwall of the Lafayette Brook ravine.

If you would indulge my serious side for a bit.

I have contemplated the following questions over the past several months. Why was the Emily Sotelo story so much more notorious than all of the other tragedies in 2022? There are very few that achieved national attention like she did. Was it because she was so young? Was it because she went missing and they found her on her

20th birthday? Was it the extreme cold that stopped SAR in their tracks? Was it because of the bad weather and each day chipped away at potential for Rescue gave way to Recovery? Was it because it could have been any one of us? Was it because many of us have gotten ourselves into trouble and we wondered why were we the ones that escaped a tragic ending?

I don't have the answer to any of these questions. No one does, that's why we keep asking them.

Many, instead, ask why didn't we hear about some of the other victims that year? Why aren't all of the fatalities national news?

Though I know this isn't national news, I'll briefly pay tribute to some of the others that did pass in 2022. June 18, Xi Chen, a 53 year old man died of exposure on Mount Clay. July 30, John R. Quick, age 65 passed away on Washington Jewel Trail, the cause is not known. August 25, Yanick Belanger, age 46, suffered a heart attack on Washington. December 12, Joseph Eggleston, age 53, fell 300 ft to death on Mount Willard, a long time resident of the area who worked on the Mount Washington Cog Railway. There was a 39 year old woman who died due to an unspecified "medical emergency" while hiking Cabot. Guppeng "Tony" Li, age 28, was located on Franconia Ridge halfway down the ridge in woods Christmas morning.

My condolences to all who have met their fate on this beautiful and sometimes unforgiving place.

I know I make light of my stumbles, bumbles and brainless maneuvers, but I am ever reminded to be humble and grateful that Mother Nature has continued to allow me to be amongst her travelers.

IN TRANSITION

I packed up my car with boxes and headed up to my new abode. It would take a couple trips like this to finish purging and packing. After unpacking the car, unpacking boxes, and loading some of my very smart house features on the phone it was time for, you guessed it, a hike!!! It was early December so it was cold, but not as much snow as is normal for that time of the year.

Nancy, my awesomest of hiking buddies, did it again. She plotted out the potential routes for a very fine hike and provided options based on the weather and how we were feeling. Thankfully, her husband lets her come out to play with me. And he has a list of all the places we could be. Leaving an itinerary is one of the many lessons we learned from those that have gone before us.

The plan was to attempt a summit of Cannon via Hi Cannon Trail. We of course discussed bail out options for not ideal weather conditions. And I said I was actually okay with planning on taking the Dodge Cutoff straight over to Lonesome Lake which was one of our bail out options. My whining might have had something to do with it, but Nancy was onboard with making the "bail out" the plan of the day.

What a delightful hike. We didn't even need traction, which is unheard of at that time of the year. We headed up the trail to the Cutoff, then onto Lonesome Lake we went. Just a dusting of snow with no other tracks in front of us, so of course I hear "where are you going?" as I trod off on my merry way off trail and to God knows where. Nancy points me back onto the trail (actually this happened long before the cutoff if truth be told, and probably more than one time.) We shared stories and sometimes walked in silence. The magic of the mountains is ever present. As we approached Lonesome Lake there were views of the Franconia Ridge poking through the trees and the splendor unfolded.

At Lonesome Lake we took some time to reflect and say goodbye to Emily. I was hoping she didn't suffer too much and I was awe-struck when gazing upon where she was found. Then, it was picture time, and lo and behold, my fingers were frozen. Another 10 seconds and it would have been frostbite time. So, onwards to the warmth of the Lodge. We broke out snacks and we both had a hot drinks. I DID remember my cocoa infused coffee this time and we enjoyed warming up and chowing down.

For the first time I decided to break out my hand warmers. I dropped them in my mittens on the way out of the hut and what a "game changer". What the hell had I been waiting for? Almost frostbite no more. After fluids in and fluids out, warm little digits, and ready to add traction to our feet, since the trail we were going down was not the same as the one we went up. A friendly fellow at the hut had come up where we were going down and encouraged the decision to micro-spike up, if you will.

The added traction was the right call, and we descended safely down the Lonesome Lake Trail. We finished up earlier than most of our usual hikes together (let's not revisit Owl's Head, suffice to say, I'm glad that's behind us) then I was to my new home. An early all you can eat stop and Nancy decided to head back home, since it's so early. Personally, I think it was more that tackling the mountain of boxes in my living room was much more intimidating than anything we've come through to date...

I headed back to Connecticut. Soon, it would be time to bring the boys home...

HOME SWEET HOME
FOR THE HOLIDAYS

Is there anything more fun than moving? Yes, anything and everything! Though I didn't always feel that way. It is amazing how quickly I can accumulate stuff.

I had retired a short time after selling my house and had spent a year purging, though that was hard to believe with all the stuff I still had. The house I was moving to was fully furnished, so all I had to do was move all the other stuff and sell all my furniture. After a very unsuccessful Estate Sale I took several car loads of stuff to Goodwill. Purge and pack and clean room by room. Then I had to isolate the cats in order to get them into carriers and ready for the big move. I had to squeeze in a quick trip to Florida to visit with Mom and my sisters. Then I could be on my way. Though I'd been doing my best to purge through the year there was just so much more.

After I returned from Florida and the final moving day was approaching it was amazing how empty the house looked, yet it was deceiving. I technically had until the end of December to move out, but a significant amount of snow was in the forecast for New Hampshire. I wanted to get up and into our new home before that happened. So early in the morning December 22nd, I made my final push to get it all complete. I kind of failed miserably. I had given the cats drugs late morning thinking I'd be ready to head out around noon but as I got close to noon, the pile of unpacked items just seemed to grow. The cleaning seemed to increase and the house seemed to grow new rooms for me to get to. Every drawer, closet door or, cabinet I opened revealed more and more items that I thought I'd already packed. I began to just throw things in the "to pack" pile and before long the pile of unpacked things grew into a mountain.

I had the cats in their carriers, which is always a harrowing ordeal, but we all survived with minimal permanent damage. Suffice to say I'm glad that the drugs had kicked in to help the process. Thankfully, a friend had called to see how I was making out. When I said "not so good" he suggested that I stay another night, but I knew that if I didn't get going that day, I wouldn't be able to get into the new driveway after the predicted snow fall.

He was my saving grace that day. I packed up the pile while he found room for everything in the car. How he managed to fit it all in is still a mystery. There was not a square inch that wasn't filled and I swear I heard the Beverly Hillbillies theme playing in the background. We left an opening so I could see the side view mirrors. At long last the three kitties, me, and all the remaining stuff were FINALLY on our way. I only stopped once along the way and we made it home a little after 10:00pm.

I brought the boys into the house, and only any necessary items needed for the night, the rest could wait. After getting the boys settled in, I passed out and woke to about eight inches of fresh snow. It continued to snow all the next day. We ended up with a couple of feet of the white stuff and I was grateful we'd made it just in time.

Luckily a neighbor had left their card for snow plowing services. I called and had my driveway plowed so I didn't have to do the shoveling was a welcome home gift to myself.

Christmas in New Hampshire was rather uneventful, well, except for the furnace kicking off on Christmas Eve. There were enough space heaters to keep us warm and toasty until we could have it fixed. We enjoyed a peaceful Christmas, put on some Holiday movies and began to settle in.

A couple days after Christmas I joined a Mount Pemigewasset hike with new and old hiking buddies. What a perfect day. Thanks for letting me join in the jaunt! This would bring up my 52WAV count. Not to mention that I got to spend time with great people and take in spectacular views. It was a great bang for your buck.

One of our party did the hike with insulated crocks. Thankfully her traction worked with the crocks. Kids - don't try this on a 4000 Footer.

I had set up a Hiking Buddies hike for Christmas Eve up Mount Pierce and potentially onto Eisenhower, but with all the snow pushed the date out, it became A Very Tortoise New Years Eve Eve Event.

The details on the event were posted as follows:

Join the Very Tortoise New Years Eve Eve winter wonderland hike up to Pierce and possibly onto Eisenhower. This is rescheduled from Christmas Eve... So, Hopefully those that wanted to make this one still can.
We can sometimes make a 1 mph pace.
As always this will be slow as we go. As always there will be huffing, puffing, wheezing and panting... Happy to stop along the way for photos, snacks, drinks, well, and just catch our breath...
This is weather dependent.

Please be prepared with your 10 essentials plus winter gear. Better yet, check out the Redline Guiding 13 essentials as listed on https://redlineguiding.com/about/resources/

We will start this journey at the Highland Center. We'll travel 3ish miles (but who's counting) on Crawford Path to the Pierce Summit. Though it is true, no hike up a 4000 Footer is easy, this is definitely one of, if not, the least hard one out there. We will assess at the Pierce Summit how everyone feels about continuing.

If you're short on holiday cheer, this gem will help get you in the spirit.

Total round trip will be approx. 6 miles with 2400 ft elevation gain if we are successful with Pierce. OR Total round trip will be approx. 9 miles with 3200 ft elevation gain if we decide to tack on Eisenhower.

I'll be watching the weather and providing updates as the time approaches. If you've never been on a Buddy Hike and want to try out winter hiking, this would be a great one for you join.

Feel free to ask questions or provide input for the group. We will stay together and go as slow as the slowest person. That would be me.

The Post hike Post went onto Facebook as follows:

What was originally planned for Christmas Eve got rescheduled on New Years Eve Eve and I'm so glad it did.

Who: Abbie Jo, Nancy, Kerri, Jocelyn, Natalie, Alicia, Beth, Laurie, our token male Paul, and Rhonda, in other words Hiking Buddies

What: Another Awesome Hike
Where: Mount(s) Pierce and Eisenhower
When: New Years Eve Eve
Why: Why not?

We had ANOTHER Great Hiking Buddies Crew. Some First time Hiking Buddies and some first time winter in the Whites hikers joined the adventure. And to make things even grander we met the one and only Eric Todd Sweet (aka Candyman, and other fine aliases) with his posse. But as per Mr. Sweet, he swept in and was gone in a flash, spreading his ever love for these great mountains to what he fondly refers to as his tramily.

We started with nine as we headed out from the AMC Highland Center. Great thing about starting from the Highland center, indoor plumbing, yes, I know, the write-up is supposed to be about the great outdoor adventure. But really, starting a good trek with an empty bladder without having to expose ourselves to the elements at the beginning of a hike up a 4000 Footer definitely has its advantages.

The first lesson for the newbies was regarding pace. I expressed what they were to expect with denoting descriptions in order from "fastest to slowest" of the slow paces. This of course is a listing of my own making, Turtle, Sloth, Snail, last but not least is Abbie Jo pace. We of course would be going Abbie Jo pace.

We did move a bit quicker than that to cross Rt 302, then onto the trail. As we hit the junction to Clinton Rd, we heard someone cry out "are you the hiking buddies?" We picked up the final member of our group rounded us out to 10. We rejoiced!

What to say about the trail conditions? It was sticky with an emphasis on "icky", and slippy footing, with mash potato consistency for the most part. Luckily there was no balling of the snow on our microspikes. We all wore traction, which was helpful, and mostly necessary. There was plenty of post holing that happened before, during, and after our travel down the trail. I don't think that even if everyone had been wearing their snowshoes it would have helped.

We had plenty of view teasers through the trees along the way. What made it a perfect day was the company. I loved listening to the conversations and enjoyed how new friendships were forged as we pushed on to our first destination. As we approached Pierce's summit, the fog bank gave an eerie feeling that perhaps Sasquatch WAS in the Whites. As the trees shrunk in stature, the temps began to drop and you could hear the wind calling. This let us know it was time to put on a layer or two before leaving the shelter of the trees, even at their stunted stature.

Then onward through the slush, I mean, who expects slush on the top of a 4000 Footer in late December? Not us, and soggy footed, we arrive. I whooped, only to be informed that we still had further to go. And sure enough I was fooled by cairn #1. Right around the bend we DID summit. Where all those that had passed us along the trail were enjoying their victory snacks. We took our summit pictures and ever so briefly the clouds opened up and we got a few views.

Thanks again to Nancy for sharing some chocolate treats for all. Eight went on to summit Eisenhower, while two of us retreated. Nancy and I retreated, and again, I was glad to do so. The hike was just enough to have gotten out and we were blessed with some peak-a-boo views on our way down. The rest of the gang had a great trip up to Eisenhower and there were so many amazing pictures that it was hard to down select.

Thank you all for joining the Creep this fine day!

ALMOST MOOSILAUKE

I had been wanting to hike Moosilauke for several years so it was time to give it a go. I posted the following in Hiking Buddies to see if I could get a group together.

The Event details were as follows:

Join The Tortoise Take-on and The Moose. It's time to come out of your shells and join some Buddies taking it slow and steady up to Moosilauke. We usually average a 1 mph pace including time to catch our breath, gawk, take pictures, eat snacks, and just enjoy our surroundings and one another's company.

This is weather dependent.

Please be prepared with your 10 essentials plus winter gear. Better yet, check out the Redline Guiding 13 essentials as listed on https://redlineguiding.com/about/resources/

We will start this journey at the Glencliff Trail up Moosilauke Carriage Road to the Moosilauke Summit.

Total round trip will be approx. 7.8 miles with 3300 ft elevation gain.

I'll be watching the weather and providing updates as the time approaches. If you've never been on a Buddy Hike and want to try out winter hiking, this would be a great one for you join.

Feel free to ask questions or provide input for the group. We will stay together and go as slow as the slowest person. That would be me...

The post hike post was as follows:

Sometimes it's an adventure just getting to the adventure. I like to arrive to the trailhead about a half hour early. I have become one of those "blindly trust google maps gps system to get me wherever I need to go."

Despite the fact that I know DESIREE (Driving EStimated Information Reliable Enough Entity) will sometimes lead me astray, like sending me down roads that don't have an outlet so I end up driving in circles because she'll continue to bring me to the same spot. I still blindly trust her to find the best route and give me an estimate of when I will arrive at my destination.

That happened to be the case once more once more. Yes, I blindly followed DESIREE to the Moosilauke meeting place. After layering up, eating a good breakfast, hydrating (hopefully early enough to do a final relieve to bladder before heading out and not have to pull over on the side of the road to find a relief spot and not lose time), check for the 15 essentials (yes, 10 as noted by AMC, 13 as listed on the Redline Guiding sight, but the additional 2 are things that are just for the ladies, set of dry things to change into after the hike, and load everything into the car, put the coordinates into DESIREE and let her do her thing. We were given intel by Tammy to make sure we had the correct trailhead because the gps will sometimes direct you to a different location. I had the correct destination location loaded. Confident that the final destination was indeed correct I proceed to follow the blue path on the screen and listen to DESIREE's gentle voice telling me where to turn.

I enjoyed the drive through the mountains as I always do. We were on track to be there 30 minutes early and according to DE-SIREE we were 8 ½ miles away when she instructed us to turn. We immediately passed two houses, one on either side of the road, but then the road looked unplowed after that and went pretty much straight up into the forest. Hmmm, I felt a bit uneasy at the remoteness and about 30 yards in I saw a sign 'steep and narrow road.' Which, one could see, but that's when the little voice in my head said "ummm, I don't think this is such a good idea. Maybe we should look for another way."

I stopped going forward, put the car in reverse, because yes, the road is actually too narrow to do a three-point turn. There were ditches on either side and my rear-view camera had become mucked up. I had to back up the old fashioned way, but of course as I turned my body to look behind me, the wheel follows suit, and I found myself sinking into the ditch and wheels spinning as I tried to launch myself back into the roadway. The more I panicked, the more the wheels spun, the more stuck I got. All of a sudden, a calm broke over me, the voice that suggested that we should not go forward (yes, there are several voices and sometimes I remember to listen to the quiet one instead of the others) says, "stop, you grew up driving in the snow, just go slow, inch your way out."

Voilà, we're out of the ditch. Yes, we in this case was me and the voices. We pull up the map and plot our OWN route. A half hour later we roll into the parking lot with all the buddies ready to go. OK, most of the buddies, ready to go…

Now onto the real story of Another mountain not summitted.

I had been trying to get up to the summit of Mount Moosilauke since I started my 4000 Footer journey. So, at least four years at the time. Therefore the Hiking Buddies event was created. Those that know me know that I don't have a problem waiting for a good weather, or at least, a reasonably not dangerous day. After a couple re-schedules, we had a day with little wind (it has been stated that there is ALWAYS wind on Moose) with forecast for light snow. Several brave souls decided they would join along.

After my late arrival we got started on the trail. I had only hiked with one of the Buddies previously, so I was happy to know someone already, and I think we had two new Hiking Buddies, who I hope enjoyed the journey to join or create more buddy hikes of their own.

There was a lot of discussion about footwear. Traction, no traction, snowshoes, bring them or not. Well, not having traction was not an option at that time of the year. Then the question was how much and when do you don said traction? I opted to leave my snow shoes behind, as did we all to start, but the conditions had been weird. The conditions were more what one expects to experience in the spring, or what is referred to as shoulder season. No, I don't know why it's called shoulder season either, hopefully some kind soul reading this will explain. When I hear that term I look over at my shoulder hoping that the answer comes to me, but then I wonder if I have dandruff or then develop a crick in my neck, and sigh and figure one day I will understand. Yes, I know I'm off track again, sorry. I do get easily distracted, even by my own thoughts.

As we started, one of our crew decided that they were going to wear their snowshoes after all. They went back and retrieved and put on said snowshoes while a majority of the group decided to put on (or already had on) their microspikes. I chose to bare boot it at that time. So, we had pretty much everything going on. There was a blanket of snow which was just warm enough to stick and ball onto some of the microspiked folks. At least one other decided to join my bare naked boots. As we continued to climb the ice under the snow became more prevalent so some put their traction back on, then we went further and they took it off, then put it on, THEN I FINALLY joined the crew and put mine on too.

It was snowing the whole time we hiked which gave a wonderful winter wonderland feel. One of my favorite times to be out on the trails. I never get tired of the way the snow clings to the trees and provides that refreshing crunch underfoot. As if you are walking on magic. This lasted until about a half mile or so from the first mountain summit of the day. That would be South Peak. It was a bit off the route to Moosilauke, I still wanted to go, just to say I'd been there.

We reached the junction, took the turn to South Peak and we got ready for more up. It was about this time that the trail conditions got even more 'not so much funnish. There had been post holing while the snow was really more like slush, which by the time we hiked had iced back over. So, ankle twist catchers I like to think of them as, which were now covered with a couple inches of snow, so not always visible. Luckily, we all made it to the summit of South Peak with no injuries and well, no views either. Decided it was too blustery to eat on the exposed mountain top and headed back to the junction.

We took some time to fuel up, change clothes, add clothes, and/or just catch our breath. One of the crew asked if we were going onto Moose, so I said that I would like to and seemed everyone was onboard. Then some folks talked about having places to be by a certain time and I had to break their bubble about the pace we were doing and that it wasn't likely to get any better as I usually take longer on the descent than I do going up, if you can imagine, yes, even slower...

So, we agreed that we would break into a few groups. Tammy was a good sport and got stuck with the Abbie Jo pace as we headed up towards the next goal. Not too far along team #2 stopped and I thought was just making a call, so Tammy and I passed that person by. We went on and met up with Samia who was waiting for her team#2 teamate. I decided to check messages and glad I did, it stated that person was headed down. Tammy took a step up to the plate and descended with our solo return. Biggest thing I emphasize on the buddy hikes I organize is that no one is ever left behind or left alone. I also had a lesson learned for me to ask if there's anyone that wants to turn around, because I can always come back another day. The mountain will be there.

We were back to three teams but now Samia was with me and onward we went. After probably a half mile or so, we assessed the time, our condition, and realizing that there was still a mile to the summit. We decided to turn around and thankfully Samia helped suggest that I take in some more nourishment at the junction. As we approached the junction, team #1 caught back up to us. I was happy to hear that they had a successful summit.

I was also happy that Samia and I got to bond. Always love making a new friend thanks to hiking buddies. And I was super happy that we turned around when we did. Gave us the opportunity to enjoy a spectacular sunset on the way down.

In conclusion, the trail may have been shit but company rocked. Moosilauke, I will be back...

Thanks again to Hiking Buddies NH48!

HIKING 2023 BEGINS WITH A BANG

In January, I started my new life in New Hampshire with a ton of fun and learning all the advantages of winter hiking. I had purchased snowshoes in the Fall of 2022 and began to put them to good use. The January post hike write-ups were largely written for Facebook and translated as best I can without the pictures that I used to go with them.

1/8/2023 Mt. Israel

Hiking Buddies Hike led by Jennifer, Michele, Nancy, Kathy (new)

Fantastic Hike Beautiful Day!

Thanks Jennifer for doing a fabulous job posting and organizing an amazing Buddies' Hike. Perfect weather with old and new friends.

I felt like Moses. Not because I could part the sea, or found tablets with directions from the holy one, or saw a burning bush. It was because I have found my people and we are free. Free to enjoy the splendor that only hiking in the White Mountains can provide.

We laughed, we cried (ok, maybe that was just me, with an overwhelming feeling of gratitude), we sang (ok, maybe just me again), we laughed some more, we took pictures, we took layers off, we put layers on, we said inappropriate things to the very handsome solo hiker (okay, that was most definitely just me), and had an overall stellar day.

I learned a new word from my long lost hister (hiking sister). Thanks Michele! There were more than 10 that signed up for the hike, so we split up into a faster and slower turtle paced group. I'll give you three guesses as to which group I was in. Yes, the third group, of course we had an Abbie Jo paced group which Michele tried to bust free from, so we tripped her at the summit so there would be no more of that. Of course we didn't trip her, but we did take lots of pictures and laugh along with her. Yes, we made sure she was okay first.

Seriously, that was the most beautiful hike I've been on this winter, hence, this year. Can you believe 2023 is here and in full force? I think I'm still in shock that I get to live in this amazing place and befriend these amazing people, doing this thing called life.

It was determined that there is a need for gaiter garters. I wonder if Steve would sell them in the Mountain Wanderer Book Store?

It was noted that I think we all started hiking the same way. Thinking we could throw on a pair of sneakers and start walking in the woods. $5000 later...

Thank you my histers for another awesome adventure.

1/11/2023 – North & Middle Sugarloaf

This solo hike was stunning.

I decided to give solo hiking another go. I picked a perfect weather day and something not too far from home. There was a little bit of a road walk but going through the campground gave me some peeks at the peaks I was hiking and I was pulled into the magic of the mountains.

I shared my Garmin Mini2 link with a couple people and this gave them and me some peace of mind. The view of the Presidential Range from both North and Middle Sugarloaf was breathtaking. I did not wander too far down the ledges but stuck just to the main trail and I was not disappointed.

This was the first location that I began my "lunchtime views" series. I will often post the view as I enjoy luch atop a mountain, in the woods, or on the side of a riverbank. Almost always a view of my outdoor exploits.

I did not see anyone until I was headed back down. I met Dave (though on a later hike called him by the wrong name) from the Almost Moosilauke hike with his dog Cooper.

1/17/2022 Prospect Mountain

Today's adventure was brought together by the Pemi Valley Hikers.

Though not a very mighty mountain, it did its best to kick my ass. There were plenty of ice flows to navigate. No pictures of the ice flows as I was just trying hard to not fall. There was enough up to put me into a wheezing, panting, and heart racing stupor as I did my best to not fall too far behind the group.

There were biscuits for Biscuit (the dog), though she did her best to beg for more tasty treats (i.e. our lunches.) And one of the crew was gracious enough to share some cappuccino chocolates, which along with my cocoa infused coffee, helped me keep pace with the group on the way down. Our hard work paid off and we enjoyed delightful vistas as we ate lunch.

One hiker's thermos tried to jump off the ledge and we tried to get Biscuit to retrieve it for him. But, Biscuit was not a retriever but a pointer, and well, she just let us know where it landed.

Thankfully we avoided the ice flows on the way down and instead tracked along a beautiful stream with spectacular ice forms. I think it was one of the other member's that found the angel's wings in the icy stream. This showed us what the beauty of nature can provide. We also saw the devastation that the force of nature can do, with several trees uprooted only a couple of weeks earlier. In the same section of the woods we experienced the exquisite ice forms and the extraordinary trauma that put us in awe.

The White Mountains do not disappoint.

And another wonderful group of friends that I can't wait to hike with again.

1/21/2023 Mount Roberts and Faraway Mountain

Another new group of amazing hiking friends that I hadn't met yet. And just at my speed! Thank you, Denise for organizing and Michele for letting me know about the Pemi Valley Hikers. It seems every time I turn around there's another wonderful community to be part of. Thanks for letting me join!

Though I was happy for the later start time, I was a bit grumbly about the late finish time. And only because I failed to see what I was getting myself into. I figured a 52WAV and additional peak. How hard could that be? Well, it was a splendid workout. Amazing views and the trail was top notch. But as always I bring my dragging ass self, so there's that.

It was exciting to have snow so that I could break out the snowshoes for the first time this year! Well, except for the extra weight, and attaching the things to a full winter backpack. And have I told you that I'm slow?

I was super excited to hike with one of my favorite histers, Ms. Michele. We each only had one fall each, but who's counting. Oh, I guess I am. Thankful for winter and the soft landings. No, there is no photo of my fall, for mine came after dark and let's say by then my mood resembled the light of day, or lack thereof. However, my mood quickly changed when I remembered to look up and out after getting back on my feet. Once I did I could see the twinkle of distant lights and the even more bright twinkling of the stars above, then focused on how the snow appeared like a billion tiny diamonds reflecting in the light of my headlamp and as I did I begin to smile again. I mean, who else is so lucky to be immersed in such an amazing experience? It is humbling.

Everyone decided to start the hike with microspikes, which made sense at first since the roadway was packed snow. We started in two groups, with the first going out ahead while a few of us waited for the folks that had to brave the longer and more treacherous commute from Mass. Oh, how grateful that my 3 plus hour commutes (one way) to seize the day are behind me. Lucky for us Denise knew a shortcut, so we stepped off the packed snow and onto the trail, where we clomped through the snow for a while until we were reunited with our crew. Most of team 1 had transitioned to snowshoes. When they caught up to us, team 2 took their lead and switched to snowshoes. And this is where the age old question comes into play How much snow warrants the use of snowshoes to help break out the trail? The answer for me is "why the $#@! didn't I do it right from the beginning?" Using snowshoes helps improve my stride, well, except when I step on myself, then try to pick up the trapped shoe. Then try hard to not lose my balance while cursing at myself, then which leg do I lift, and as my arms spin wheel try not to stab thy neighbor with my poles. But, yeah, snowshoes are much better. Ahhhh…

Someone we passed (note, we did not catch them and pass them, they were going in the other direction, hence they were completing their hike as we were beginning ours) asked how we liked using the snowshoes as opposed to strapping on crampons. For those that don't know what crampons are, well, imagine the teeth on a bear trap, now strap those to the bottom of your feet and try walking. Great for sticking to icy trails, but also great for slicing a gash in ones own leg, or tripping on an exposed rock or root.

Personally, because I tend to be pigeon toed, I find that the snowshoes help me open up my stance and improve my stride. Well, except for the occasional stepping on ones-self, see above… They are kind of fun, like how the pioneers must have felt traipsing across the countryside. Visions of Jeremiah Johnson dance across my mind. Though at the end of the day, we get to stop at McDs for your favorite burger instead of having to shoot, track, catch, skin, build a fire, and cook some poor wildlife and get up the next morning to do it all over again…

Team 1 went on ahead while my fellow turtles and I proceeded at a more optimal rate. That way we got to chat with each other. And talk about upcoming adventures, like riding the snow cats up the Auto Road and snowshoeing or skiing down. Which sounds like an awesome thing to do, not having to work to do the up, and also having the option to just stay in the toasty warm vehicle to bring us back down if conditions are less than ideal. During the discussion one of our party, I'll call her Party A, stated that her husband was against it. To which I responded, that's why I don't have one of those (no, of course that's not why, but really we could write a whole book about THAT). Party B chimed in, "me either, though I do have a list of friends that I go down when I need help doing things, like opening the pickle jar."

Eureka! A list of friends to help me around the house. That's brilliant! OK, just leave me a message if you want to get added to my list.

My fellow histers always have the best ideas.

So, the only real challenge to hiking with snowshoes going up a mountain is the fact that, well, you still have to go up the mountain. The more aggressive mountaineering snowshoes have these devices called televators. What is a televator you may ask. Well, it raises your heel, so if you are going up a steep incline, then your foot can step as if you are on a flat surface. But you need a steep enough incline for it to be helpful, otherwise you just make your snowshoes into tennis rackets with heels. And, while I'm not graceful to begin with, just put me in heels and well, let's just say the result is not pretty. And really who the Sam Hell came up with heels in the first place and why do we still wear them? Anyways, after heels up, heels down, stop to rest, a snack at the lookout, where my dear friend Michele got some very awesome photos of me in my natural state of 'what am I doing? where am I going? who the hell am I? what am I doing (again)? Then Oh, the camera's on. Smile...' more heals up, heels down, climb, climb, climb, we finally arrived at the summit of Mount Roberts.

I took off my warm fuzzy hat. I proceeded to feel like cousin IT as my "poker straight" hair tumbled into my face.

Team 1 made it to the summit of Mount Roberts about a half hour before Team 2. We took time to enjoy the summit, eat, and decide who was going back and who was continuing on to Faraway. Daisy May, the pupper in the group started to make some not so happy growly sounds, which indicated that it was time to move on.

I joined the group hiking to Faraway, which indeed felt far away for this slug of a hiker. On the trek over, I discovered that there was another badge, hence list, of mountains to keep track of. Another list to add to my 4000 Footers, 52 WAVs and now the Ossippee Range. Ugh...

Who am I kidding? I LOVE another list. Time to set up spreadsheets to track progress, maybe some bar charts, or pie charts or pivot charts. Sort by distance, time, elevation, how many times one fell, number of expletives used. Oh, the possibilities are endless. Oooo, maybe I could add charts to my write-ups? I know some of you are rolling your eyes right now and probably thinking "noooo, I think your write-ups are too long, and most probably off topic, already."

It was a very winter wonderlandy walk, even if it was far away to our next summit. Michele impressed us with her bushwacking skills. OK, truth be told, she just said, "eff it" and went straight up the double back section that brought us to the turn off. Under the chain link fence, which wasn't as easy as it sounds, and onto our second summit of the day. More snacks and a bit of a rest before heading back.

There is something especially magical about sunsets in the mountains. The mix of colors, gold, red, blue, orange and the fading of the light, with that last bright glow as the sun disappears is so very peaceful. Like getting tucked into bed with a kiss goodnight.

Alas, when I got in the car and prepared to drive away, Michele called out "headlamp." And sure enough, I was tucked in and ready to hit the road with my headlamp still on my head and blaring.

1/24/2023 – Chapel Rock and Pine Mountain

Well, if you are in need of a good workout, just head out and break trail.

I met another wonderful new hiking buddy, well, actually we met during my First official Hiking Buddies hike, but this was our first hike together. Had an awesome day breaking trail.

There's a good reason why this is called Pine Mountain…

There were plenty of pictures that show that I am a tree hugger. OK, yes, I was just using it to try and get back on my feet. Holy crap, that was waaaayyyy harder than it should have been. Thankfully my partner in crime was there to get the photos. And this is another reason why solo hiking, especially in a remote area probably isn't the greatest idea for me. I can see the headlines now… Woman's body found, she was hugging a tree, not sure how long it took her to finally succumb to the futility of it all. We do know the Gray Jays had a mighty feast. RIP…

We had to use the televators on the snowshoes, but because the terrain would be steep only for periods of time, wish they were called teleporters and they would just bring us up the mountain.

1/28/2023 – Tecumseh Buddies Hike

Thanks Jennifer for doing another spectacular job setting up another great event!

Hiking Buddies NH48 buddies are just the best! Thank you to all those that had broken trail before we got there. I got to give my snowshoes a free ride during the hike. That's OK, they deserved the rest, after all they'd gotten a lot of use during the week and even snowshoes deserve to have some fun.

This hike had been rescheduled from the week before. And quite frankly I was kind of doing a cheer because with the winter road closures, my commute would be an additional half an hour longer. But when my friend said she wanted to go play with her friends in the mountains, I knew it was on.

Prior to us arriving the infamous John, who was always prepared, had offered up a waterproof pouch for a phone. I put in my bid and was awarded the gift. However, when I went to slide in my phone, found out that it wasn't slim enough, and much like me trying to squeeze my booty into my underlayers in the winter found out that yes, that waterproof pouch did make my phone look fat. And though with much determination, that sucker did get squeezed in, trying to get it out was as difficult to do as when taking a bio break and having, use your imagination…

There was a bigger group that got split up so that the tortious of us could hang back without the pressure.

We had a Hiking Buddies virgin among us. So, the turtles that stayed behind were myself, the incomparable Miss Nancy, the indescribable John Prepared for Any Eventuality, our Ring Leader Jennifer and The Virgin.

Had a great time playing with my friends in the snow. Though Nancy and I hung back with John to have a little picnic lunch and cheer on those coming and going.

Thankfully John carries everything one could need for just about anything that could happen. He was the official trail angel and cheerleader of Tecumseh. Patching up the sketchiest boot/traction combo I have ever seen. I think it was mostly zip ties holding a bit of rubber and couple pieces of metal to the bottom of some work boots. John received the MacGyver award for the day.

Overall outstanding day with awesome buddies.

1/31/2023 – Stinson Mountain

A bit chilly and an awesome day with The Pemi Valley Hikers.

Thanks for joining us Molly, that was the pupper of the group. Sorry that I forgot the name of the two legged animals that I met.

No, I'm not really sorry since Molly was the cutest! She was quick to sniff out who had the best snacks and began shamelessly begging. I think that's why we bonded, since I do the same thing. Yes, if we're hiking together and you bring goodies beware of my doe eyes, I can indeed look quite pathetic.

I was the only one that opted for snowshoes. I am not sorry or ashamed (see just like Molly) of that decision. Served me well when stepping "off trail."

Thank you Jon for making sure I was OK, and hanging back with me as I shlogged my way uphill. With as often as I get out I keep hoping that I don't always sound like a broken tea kettle as I wheeze my way on any incline and need to stop every 10 feet. OK, it's probably longer, but feels like not very far.

Even over my labored breathing and snowshoe crunching we could hear the wind roaring and were a bit nervous about emerging onto the summit. Surprisingly enough we were greeted with a calm, sunny, and delightfully frigid wonderland. The views were amazing and the trees were covered in ice and icicles that made them look as if someone had decorated them by hand and we were just waiting for the flashing lights to enhance their beauty. Actually, nothing manmade could have come close to nature's decorations as we encountered them. The pictures didn't do it justice, and of course it reminded me of why I work so hard to push my body and work my lungs sometimes past their breaking point.

We took some time to enjoy a picnic in the snow and listened to football talk. Now if we'd thought to bring our sleds, well the descent would have been much quicker, but probably not all that safe. Even without the sleds, going down was much more aaahhh.

Thanks again for making this possible Pemi Valley Hikers!

TIME TO SKI

Hiking up mountains isn't the only fun activity in the North Country.

Nancy asked and I answered.

"Skiing?"

"Yes!"

We decided to check out Bretton Woods. Well, only I was checking it out since Nancy was already a fan. It was a short distance from my place and Nancy touted that they have the best groomed trails around. I was definitely in.

It had been a looooong time since I hit the slopes. The last time I went skiing, I had come home to a pipe rupture in my home. The result was an eight month process of an unplanned re-model. Not a recommended way to get a new kitchen.

I had brand new ski boots from four years ago. The price tag was still on the boots and they had never been put to use. I rented a pair of skis and was ready to go. We went into the lodge where Nancy and I found a nice place to get ready to hit the trails.

The toughest part of the day was trying to get those damn ski boots on. I pulled the front away from the back of the boot opening with all my strength, but it was like trying to pry open a gator's clamped jaw. No give, and what little progress I made, would get undone as soon as I tried slipping my foot into the opening.

I tried it sitting, standing and stomping, and each time couldn't get my heel to drop in. I tried my left foot, right foot, stand up, sit down, pull, pull, swear, stand up and stomp, much more cursing, but to no avail. Just as I was ready to give up and had planned to see if the ski rental crew could help, Nancy came to the rescue. She grabbed the front of the opening, put all her weight into it and pulled while I stood up and pushed my foot in with all my might. I was almost afraid that my heel would break, since the boot wasn't giving and then all of a sudden it gave just enough and my foot dropped into the bottom. Success!!! Then she helped me with the other boot. Whew!

The man at the table next to us, had a similar struggle. I nodded over to him, and we agreed that it was quite a workout. I was almost ready to call it a day. Instead, we finished putting on all our layers, then realized that I didn't have my helmet, so I clomped off to the ski rental space which was down a flight of stairs. Walking in ski boots is like having cement blocks for shoes. I know, we never wore helmets back in the day, but I was not willing to go without my noggin protected. Another workout done, wasn't sure if I'd have enough in the tank to actually ski after that.

Finally, coat, gloves, scarf, helmet and goggles and we were off. Besides that awesome feeling of flying, the views from the top of the mountain were more amazing than from any other ski area I had been to.

I had forgotten how fun skiing was. That feeling of flying, when you're right on the edge of being out of control. It is fun that is, as long as no one falls down or has to walk back uphill in ski boots. Hoofing back up to a missed turn in ski boots is NOT the same as hiking up a mountain with snowshoes on. Another something I don't recommend.

Life is excellent!

MORE WINTER WONDER THROUGHOUT FEBRUARY

After looking at my maps and going through the White Mountain Guide, I decided to try one of the many trails nearby. Would this be the start of my tracing the White Mountain Guide? Some people still call it Redlining. When I asked what is redlining, someone told me to open up my White Mountain Map and sure enough all of the trails were in red. Hence, the term "red"lining. Therefore, when someone says they're are redlining it means they are on a mission to hike each and every trail listed in the White Mountain Guide. Afterwards, I became aware that this term has a racial connotations to it. Philip Carcia, better known through his blog Finding Philip, does a great job of explaining why, so I will just note that from here on I will refer to trying to hike all the trails listed in the White Mountain Guide as tracing.

I was onto another list, with my meager beginning on the White Trail up to Crows Nest. I wanted something manageable, so I started with a two mile and 650 ft elevation gain trip. I was pretty sure there

186

wouldn't be anyone else out there. I drove down North Road (yes, everyone up in Gorham expects that you know where that is) to the Philbrook Farm Inn. I found the little lot that the Inn keeps plowed out just for hikers, which I think is pretty sweet of them. There was only one set of snowshoed steps so at least I knew where to start. I did have to do some navigating, as the other set of prints went off on another trail only a few hundred feet into my journey. We'd see how well my MapQuest (navigation app) worked. I did have a proper paper map, just in case, but I was able to make my way with my phone navigation app.

It was a nice day for a little trail breaking. I really wanted to follow all the creatures' footprints I came across. Until I WAS following what was most likely a couple of coyote tracks. Then, I got a bit nervous when I thought I heard growling behind me. I spun around, which isn't really that easy in snowshoes and you're sunk into a foot or so of snow. I raised my hiking poles up and was ready for a battle. After my heart rate was pounding in my ears and I was ready for the confrontation, I realized that it was the sounds of snowmobiles down in town and not a rabid coyote out to get me.

As I laughed at myself, I continued on and admired the rest of the critter tracks and wondered where they all went. I was up and back on a beautiful day with no further encounters real or imagined.

A couple days later someone told me to go take a hike, so I did and I brought my hiking buddy, now friend, Lisa, with me. We decided to hike up Mount Pemigawasett and had another awesome day on the trails.

When the mountains call, we listen. That was the perfect girls' day out. Even though the snow on the trail was packed down, I chose to snowshoe it. The only down side to wearing my snowshoes, is the stinking noise that they make. There was an awful lot of "what"s going on as my friend tried talking to me. I was so excited that we broke a 1.1 mph pace. I almost felt like a trail runner. :-D

We took in the views at the summit and had a little snack. That's when I discovered that my new microlight thermal drinking container leaked like a sieve. And then I knew why it was on sale. Grrr. The worst part about it was that about a quarter of my beloved mock mocha was gone. Now my pack is a shade darker than it was and I must apologize to the LNT community for leaving a dark brown stain on the summit of the mountain. At the same time my beautiful friend's drink fell over, leaving a bright red stain, so don't be surprised if you are atop Mount Pemigewasset and it appears that you've run across a crime scene. It was just us, Frick and Frack of the spillage.

After having the summit all to ourselves, and our spillage, we headed from whence we came. Along came the puppers and their human kind. One of the humans was going up on a big tired bike. One of the human and pupper pair passed us twice, making it to the summit and back to the parking lot before we got back down.

As we approached the parking lot we discovered how much we both love the theater and now we have another topic to discuss on our next adventure. If you hear poorly executed show tunes out in the Whites, well it's probably just us.

We made it to our vehicles just in time to see the headlights of the snowmobile parade approach. And we were grateful for having gone up early.

MOUNT WASHINGTON SHENANIGANS

When your hister lets you know there's a group event for Snow-coach up and Snowshoe down Mount Washington adventure and asks if you want to join, the only logical answer is "Hell ya!"

It was an all ladies event that started at Great Glen Trails. This is where we met to board the snowcoaches. I was looking forward to catching up with Michele on the snowcoach ride up the mountain. I didn't realize that we were assigned to different vehicles. Then, it felt a bit like getting on the school bus and trying to find a seat.

My initial disappointment about not getting to ride with Michele quickly vanished as I realized we wouldn't have been able to hear each other talking over the droning of the snowcoaches anyway. I did my best to enjoy the ride, but boy oh boy it wasn't a smooth or quiet one. To make matters worse I was in the furthest seat to the rear, so it was extra bumpy. It felt like we were being pulled by a kicking mule the whole way.

Even though we were bounced around, it was still a great way to experience at least part of Mount Washington. I hadn't experienced being on the mountain itself yet, despite the fact that I had moved to the area several months earlier. The snowcoach brings people up the Auto Road in the winter, while the road is closed to regular traffic. Even with the four tracks that are used instead of wheels for traction, the snowcoach can only go up the mountain so far.

The snowcoaches stopped and we all got out and had some incredible views. The drivers had to wait to hear back from their scout whether they could go further up the mountain. After the drivers got word that the road ahead was okay for travel, we were like kids on a field trip and the snowcoach drivers were like chaperones. They had a Dickens of a time gathering us all back together. Before getting back on our respective vehicles, Michele and I had discussed whether we wanted to hike back from that point or further up the mountain. There was just enough of the notorious Mount Washington winter wind to help us decide that we were okay not having to start higher up where it was more exposed, hence, more winter wind. The blusteriness we were feeling right there was more than enough of the infamous Washington winter weather for us.

The snowcoach drivers were successful and we all got aboard again and up a bit further we went. When we got as far as we would go the drivers let us all out and about half of the riders decided to hike from that point. We took a moment to take in the views from above and confirm that we were making the right decision to start snowshoeing down from our first stopping spot.

We got back to the lower spot and disembarked and watched the snowcoaches head back down to go fill themselves up with more silly people that enjoy playing in the snow and cold of the beautiful beast. Not only are Michele and I considered turtle hikers, I suppose we are also considered turtle "get our shit togetherers" as well. I did have my snowshoes on fairly quickly, but only because of all the practice I had been getting and they were now like a part of me. A snowshoe appendage if you will. As Michele found somewhere to sit and get her snowshoes on I took the opportunity to water the stumpy trees. As you may have gathered by now, my bladder is probably the size of a walnut.

It was about that time that I realized my bandana was missing. A very necessary item in the winter, runny noses must be managed. Before I headed to the shrubbery Michele let me borrow her bright orange bandana so she should keep track of me. No running off on her she said, yeah, because we all know how fleet a snowshoer I am. All I could think about was how I was failing the LNT community once again as I was sure my yellow bandana was fluttering down the mountain probably snagged on a little spruce or the like by then.

I returned and we were both suited up and ready to go. The rest of the gang had started on their way so it was just us chickens. The first thing we did was get photos by the "USE LOW GEAR" sign, as if we have any other gear.

Then Michele decided to take a video of me. I have no idea what I was thinking, but I was trying to act out how windy it was. I thought I was looking tough, fighting against the wind. I imagined a great show of a winter wonder woman fighting her way across the frozen tundra. That was decidedly NOT what I looked like, and any thoughts of acting should not be included as my next line of work. Instead, I heard a roar of laughter erupt from my friend as I went over to her and we watched the video. Instead of a winter heroine I look like a moose calf on unsteady feet, with a loaded diaper, if a moose calf wore a diaper that is. Not exactly the look I was going for, but entertaining none the less.

Then downward we continued. Stopping to gaze at the mighty peaks around us. It was a spectacularly beautiful day and blue bird skies abounded; it showed off the snowy peaks all around us. We decided to take the side trip to Low's Bald Spot. A little jaunt that would provide unobstructed views of the tallest peaks in the Whites. It was a little extra work to get up to the spot, but we were troopers and we were not disappointed.

After going up we had to come down and Michele took the opportunity to show how NOT to descent a steep slope in snowshoes. She opted to butt slide and ended up, well, in a compromising position with an evergreen tree. Let's just stay that I hope Steve (her husband) doesn't get jealous very easily because that tree got to know Michele in the biblical sense, if you know what I mean.

We finally got her untangled from the tree, you know, after we stopped laughing. We needed a break after that and found the perfect perch to sit upon as we enjoyed our snacks.

After snacking we continued down the rest of the way to the Auto Road. Once we got back on the Auto Road we met with some of our crew who had opted to come down from the higher starting point. They caught up to us thanks to our side trip. We got to the bottom of the mountain where the toll is collected from the drivers when the Auto Road is open to the general public vehicles. The toll booth looks like a little house and is appropriately named Toll House, but don't you think that they should pass out chocolate chip cookies with a name like that? And really, the house is adorable.

We were in the home stretch then, just needed to cross the street and back to our own vehicles. What a perfect day. Until…

I went to get my keys, and realized the clasp that I had the keys on was still attached to my pack, but, alas, the keys were not!

Somewhere, I assume where we stopped to snack, on the side of Mount Washington is a set of keys for a Subaru Impreza. If you find them please pack them out for me. And once again the LNT community is cringing…

I called AAA because I did have a spare set of keys in my car so all they had to do was come out and break into the car for me. I could see the tag on the keys peaking out from my center counsel, so I knew they were there. It only took four hours for them to come, in the meantime my hister stayed with me as the shop at Glen Trails had closed and we waited four hours for AAA to arrive in Michele's car. The sunset was pretty amazing. What saved us from boredom was that silly video of my moose poop walk. We watched it over, and over, and over. Each time we would laugh like it was the first time we'd seen it, yet, somehow it got funnier with each viewing.

I recommend everyone find a hister and if you don't have one I'll share mine because she is simply the best.

While waiting for AAA Michel exclaimed, "I'm having hot flashes in the strangest places."

Then she started pulling hand warmers from her jacket, pants pockets, and out of her socks. You know how some women carry their phone or money next to their bosom, maybe a warmer or two were pulled from that location.

Michele did tell me that day that she was on the lookout for my somewhat crusty mountain man. Apparently, the AAA person was not it. If you think you might be him, send your application to Michele. She needs to do the vetting, since I've been told that my male companion picker is broken.

ALWAYS LEARNING

Because I truly believe that you can never be over prepared, and I want to always be learning, AND I REALLY wanted to meet Ty Gagne I decided to go to see the series of speakers titled 'SAFETY IN THE BACKCOUNTRY'. A few hiking buddies were also going to see the safety in the backcountry speakers. Christine and I decided to meet for a quick bite before. The location of the event was in Vermont, and I had thought where I moved to was 'up there'. Which it is, but the location for the speaker event was 'out there'.

The only way to get out there was on dirt roads. Even though some of the roads around us where I grew up were dirt roads, it had been a very long time since I'd had the experience of driving them. And if you think driving on a snowy road can be tricky I invite you to go ahead and find yourself some good back country, dirt roads to get the full experience, especially when they are wet.

There were a couple of good slipping and sliding spots that I thought for sure I was just going to slide right off the road and land in a ditch. Of course, there was no cell service in those remote places.

So, I just held my breath, white knuckled the steering wheel, and did my best to urge the car to go in the direction that I wanted it to go.

The little café, The Peacham Café, where I met Christine was small and rustic. The kitchen was about the same size as the dining space on the first floor, there was a loft type space upstairs that spanned the area over the kitchen. You know that it's going to be great food when you can watch who's cooking. This was home-style cooking at its best. I'm pretty sure it is the only dining establishment in a ten mile radius from Peacham Congregational Church, where the event was being held. If you happen to be in Peacham, VT or passing through, and when I say passing through, I mean within 30 miles or so, do yourself a favor stop into the café and treat yourself to a fabulous experience.

The church was just two doors down and it was a perfect venue. I still think of community when stepping into an old New England church even if I'm not there to worship. Because I've always been the nerdy type, I went right down to the first row. There's a special kind of energy that comes from people who speak about the things they are passionate about. You could feel the energy level rising as folks filtered into their pews as the electronic equipment was being tested.

I had shamelessly brought along my Ty Gagne books to be signed, if there was going to be time for that, and if he was going to be willing.

Not too long after we sat down. Christine and I noticed Ty getting his stuff ready at the front of the room. I picked up my books and went up and ask him if he was indeed Ty Gagne. I asked if he wouldn't mind signing my copies of his books. He did but nodded over to Sgt Heidi Murphy, the Assistant District 3 Chief with New Hampshire Fish and Game department and said "they are the real heroes."

I whole heartedly agree that it is the people that work Search and Rescue (SAR) that put themselves on the line to help those that find themselves in precarious situations in The Whites. However, I wouldn't realize their tireless efforts if it wasn't for Ty's books. That was how I came to understand all that are affected when the team gets called when someone is in need of help either real or imagined.

Stacy arrived before the speakers started and the four up us took our seats up front. There ended up being five speakers all together. Ty started with a story of a hike he'd done on the Franconia Ridge and all of the decisions that could have landed him in trouble. This was the thing he does, explain decision making process and how any one of us could find ourselves in trouble if unaware. After his talk he opened up a question-and-answer session for the attendees. There was a woman who identified herself as a psychologist that was kind of rude and a bit of a bully. She blasted him with questions like "why didn't you tell them how you felt? Who did you go on the hike? Why did you continue?" Then kind of just repeated the same theme on something that happened years ago.

The rest of the audience really appreciated Ty's candor and how he put himself and his story out there. The Safety event was being streamed live, so I did receive messages from other hiking buddies that couldn't attend in person. It was neat to know that so many were getting the benefit of the discussions.

After Ty the next set of speakers were Sgt Heidi Murphy and Drew Clymer, Vermont Department of Public Safety Search and Rescue Coordinator. They tag teamed their discussion presenting the difference in Vermont versus New Hampshire approach to SAR. Who takes the lead and how efforts are coordinated. It was interesting to me that New Hampshire actually has it written in the state laws that New Hampshire Fish and Game shall lead all SAR efforts in New Hampshire.

Whereas, Vermont has a civilian coordinate SAR efforts in Vermont. Both Vermont and New Hampshire call upon many of the same volunteered base groups. We learned about the Hike safe card and how those funds have greatly helped in paying for SAR efforts.

The next speaker was Jeff Lane who has worked in The White Mountains for many years including as a snow ranger, weather forecaster, rescue leader and as Avalanche predictor. Though he had a great message on preparedness regarding hiking The Whites, he kind of lost the audience with his introduction. His introduction was roughly a statement that if any of us passed him on his way to do a trail run up Adams and he just had a water bottle, but nothing else, would we say he's prepared. All of us who participated in the answer said "no." He said, that yes, he was, because it's a well traveled trail and even if something happened there would be others to take care of him or get him help. Actually, he became a bit snarky when someone asked what he'd do if he twisted his ankle, and he answered that he could crawl that far without a problem. Anyone who'd been up Mount Adams knows that wouldn't be an easy thing to do. To those of us that have read Ty's book "Where You'll Find Me…" know that his response wasn't very engaging or respectful. So, Jeff, please think about a new opening the next time you talk about safety in the Backcountry.

Last but not least Andrea Kane gave a presentation on the SOLO Wilderness Medical Training courses. It's like First Aid on steroids. Keeping everyone ever mindful that when you are in the Backcountry and there is a mishap, it may be a long time before someone can come rescue you, so the more you can do for yourself and your hiking buddies, the better. Having a top notch First Aid Kit and knowing how to use it is of the utmost importance. Unfortunately, I tend to pass out at the sight of blood. Though I still intend on taking the SOLO Wilderness First Aid Course. Maybe I'll see you there?

So much great information by a wonderful group of people. Thank you for your tireless efforts on education and training for those of us who like to play in the wild.

MORE WHITE MOUNTAIN MISCHIEF

The day after the 'Safety In the Backcountry event' I was signed up on a Hiking Buddies hike up Mount Madison. This would be my second attempt. It seemed fortuitous that the hike was titled ATTEMPT 2 Turtles Take on Mount Madison. It turned out that the second time was a charm.

A fellow Hiking Buddies turtle hiker was hosting the hike. His name was Sundarapandiya (yes, as of the time I am writing this, that still is his name.) He said to just call him Sundar and that it sounds like Thunder. Then I realized why some of my other hiking buddies called him Thunder. There ended up being five of us all together on the hike.

Thankfully Sundar's originally event was also rescheduled due to weather. And that was one reason why I felt comfortable joining his ATTEMPT 2. My kind of people go slow and take heed of the weather.

My planned attempt at Isolation scheduled for that day was thwarted, so I reached out to my usual turtles, but they all had to do that thing that people do to make a living. I have a hard time even saying (or writing) that four letter word now that I'm of the retired sector. Then changed my plans to take a second attempt at the Moose with Nancy. But, to no avail, since Nancy ditched me for a much more glamorous offer to spend the night up on Mount Washington. Well, quite frankly I would have ditched her for a more appealing offer as well, maybe...

Therefore, I was actually excited to see that Sundar's event was posted for that very same day that I was now free. And the weather report couldn't have been better. What more could a 4000 Footer bagger ask for? Bluebird sky and little to no winds with cool temps (it was still February after all.) But then again I did attend the "Safety In the Backcountry" event and began to wonder if I should go do this event with people I hadn't hiked with before. However, that really is kind of the premise of the whole Hiking Buddies FB page. Meet like minded and similar hiking type folks to be out there doing what we love to do so we're not doing it alone.

After reading the trail report and checking in with Sundar, who had hiked with some of my other regular turtles and came with a few thumbs up as another tried and true turtle, decided attempt 2 for Madison was a go. There were five of us confirmed, so I took the "long" 10 minute ride to the trailhead in the morning. After MANY trips from CT to do this amazing thing, I feel no shame in gloating about the 10 minute commute. I welcome my friends to impose upon me and stay any time you are planning on hiking up in the Whites, especially the northern presis.

We started up the Valley Way Trail. Yes, me in my snowshoes and Laura in K-10s. They are a bit more aggressive than microspikes but not actual crampons. We all talked about the previous day's safety event and re-iterated how Ty's books were instrumental in how we all approach hiking in the Whites. As we were merrily chatting along the way a couple of trail runners bounded by.

I stated to our group after they passed "I think that looked like Philip Carcia."

However, I've never met him in person, only chatted with him through FB and messenger. So, I didn't impede his descent by asking him if he was who I thought he was. Instead, I marveled at how he and his companion seemed to float by.

We continued to trudge, huff, puff, and move forward step by step. As we reached an area where we could actually see the summit from the trail we heard whooping and hollering.

We finally came out to where the Madison Hut is and took time to eat a bit before taking the final climb up the summit. Refreshed and ready, it seemed like we were floating as we reached our destination. The sun was so bright that everything was shimmering. We got to see Mount Washington in all its winter glory sparkling in the sunlight. I don't recall ever having seen anything so pristine in all my life. I know Nancy must have been enjoying the experience up on Washington as we looked over in delight.

I was truly thankful that sometimes not having reached a goal in the first time gives way to an unprecedented experience of euphoria. None of us wanted to leave the summit. We lingered for quite a while just in the beauty and feeling accomplished. I thank Hiking Buddies for coming through again.

When I got home, I took a look at FB and up popped a picture of Mount Washington taken by Philip that morning. Sure enough it was him that we crossed paths with on the trail. He also asked if we'd heard them howling when they got to the bottom. I said we did and emphasized the difference in our speed, or lack there of. For it was about a 2 ½ mile trek for them in the time we went about 500 feet. This reminds me that my journey is not a race. Philip did give me permission to trip him next time in order to say hello in person. We shall see.

The following week I took a drive down to New York City to visit a friend. She came back up to the North Country for a visit. While she was here I had a chance to show off just a glimpse of what I fell in love with. To Mount Willard we went. Before heading there though, I gave my friend from the Big Apple some homework. I asked her to read the section in the White Mountain Guide on the 10 essentials and we went through our packs to take inventory.

Though I apologize to my NYC girl if it sounded like I was treating you like a child. I will always err on the side of being too cautions when it comes to hiking in the Whites.

From the Big Apple to the Little Mountain with a Big Bang for your hike. My friend and I summited Mount Willard on a very spectacular day. Welcome to my World my friend. Hope you enjoyed!

After I was home alone again I decided to continue knocking off trails in the White Mountain Guide. I met up with another friend and we did the Red Trail, Blue Trail, Mount Cabot (not the 4000 Footer) loop. It was interesting because there was active logging going on. Not the day we were hiking because it was the weekend, but fresh tracks and lots of piled up cut down trees. Much of the trail was logging swatches cut out by heavy machinery but not along the whole route so we ended up losing the trail after a while following the logging roadish tracks.

It was quite an adventure to find where the trail took off from the logging tracks. We had to back track to find where the actual trail veered back into the woods. Thankfully I didn't try to tackle that one alone because there was a bit of water crossing and it took all three of us to find our way back to the trail and help find safe passage across the water crossing.

We did find our way, up, down, around and back again. I added those trails as complete to the list of accomplishments.

It was the end of February and time to take another try at getting to the summit of Moosilauke. Nancy agreed to meet me but when we got to the trailhead we opted to go up Blueberry Mountain instead. Another beautiful day and I ended up getting another 52WAV under my belt.

MARCH MADNESS

I started March off with another trip back to Lonesome Lake with Hiking Buddy extraordinaire. Me and my gal pal Nancy did it again and OMG it was even more delightful than the last time. We went just in the nick of time too, since the snowy days doldrums had started kicking in. I was just feeling blah and apparently Nancy was too. Like she said, it's the old, the less I do, the less I want to do cycle had kicked in. I was right there with ya Sistah. The last couple of days before our hike I spent on the couch telling myself, just one more episode of 'The Marvelous Mrs. Maisel'. But, man, oh man, all that snow sure did make everything purty.

Right from the start it was a delight, well except for the bare booters, or Post-Holers, which is most often said as a curse word. Really people, if the trail you're on in the Whites happens to be white, then snowshoes are in order. We let the post-holers pass and onward we traveled. Through the Lafayette Campground and up the Lonesome Lake Trail. The peaks on the Franconia Ridge looked close enough to touch. It was the clearest that I have ever seen the details on the ridge, it was as if every peak popped.

Every couple of steps we'd look ahead, and behind, each time gasping and stating "how beautiful!" The trees all draped with their gleaming formal wear. Every once in a while some of the snowy white powder would let loose from the treetops and it seemed as if it was snowing just for us. The whole trip up was breath-taking, and I don't just mean because we were going uphill. Even though we were going uphill, we both were more energized when we reached the lake than when we had started our trek. I think we were both down to our base layer about the time we reached the lake, with the sun shining and the trail only partially broken out, made for a good exercise to boot.

I got a couple more amazing views of the ridge from the deck of the Lonesome Lake hut. Hence, my favorite selfie spot. Nancy brought the chocolate, so we were in heaven, but all good things must come to an end and we headed back out.

We decided to head down, well really up, up, up, then an awful lot of down on Dodge Cutoff and on the Hi-Cannon Trail. We got to break out the Dodge Cut-off and followed a lone set of Post-holer tracks down Hi-Cannon. See, I bet you said it like a swear word that time, didn't you? There were a few falls, so thank goodness the snow was soft, and a few, "I'm just gonna butt slide here, because I'm gonna end up on my butt one way or the other, at least this way I have some control over it."

The truth is, when it's steep, rocky, and icy underneath, there's still not that much control no matter how you make it down. On the other hand, what a blast! It was like being a kid again and your Mom says, go outside and play, just make it home before it gets dark. "Go play in the snow," so we did.

If you're up in the North Country on a snowy day, come on out and play. Bring your snowshoes and join us for some winter wonderland fun!!!

A couple of days later I set up a snowshoe hike on Hiking Buddies. It was time for me to make peace with Lincoln Woods.

One of the Hiking Buddies administrators threw down the gauntlet, he challenged Hiking Buddies to create more events because he was disappointed at the lack of HBNH48 events posted for that Sunday. So, of course, me and my histers (hiking sisters) picked up the challenge and came through in flying colors and fits of laughter!

Thank you to my "old" buddies Nancy, Michele, and Stacy. Along with another delightful addition to our crew Diane. Yes, I made us all line up as follows: Diane, Abbie, Michele, Nancy, and Stacy (DAMS), so we could be those DAMNS hikers for the day.

First, we all had to get to the parking lot. A normal 5 minutes through the town of Lincoln to the Lincoln Woods trailhead took about a half an hour. I love that we were all apologizing for being late even though we were all stuck in the same traffic. It seems EVERYONE wanted to ski at Loon on Sunday, which I was grateful for, since my fear was that they were all going hiking.

I had rushed out the door and was well on my way when I realized that I'd forgotten to put in my contact lenses. Then about half way there I noticed that gas was running low in the car, and then it hit me that I also forgot my purse, which holds my wallet, you know where the money and credit cards are kept. Thankfully my car actually lets me know how many more miles I can drive before it's empty empty. Not like the old days where you tested to see how far the needle could go past the empty line before it was really empty.

We ended up having another fun day where we didn't act our age and played in the snow.

Best thing about hiking Lincoln Woods are the heated bathrooms located in the parking lot. OK, maybe not the BEST thing, but it's right up there. If you are a woman of a certain age or hiking with women of a certain age, you might want to keep this gem of knowledge in your back pocket. You'll be sure to impress.

Because of the extra time in the Loony traffic, all of our party headed directly to the most appreciated the heated bathroom even more than usual. Where a normal five minute section turned into a half hour commute for us all. I think my favorite group chat messages were from everyone stuck in the same traffic. I think each one of us stating that they were going to be late because they (and I mean all of us) were stuck coming thru Lincoln and past Loon. All I can say is that I'm glad we weren't skiing and that it was smooth sailing after passing the slopes. But boy, oh, boy, we had no problem finding each other, since I think we all pulled up as close as we could to the bathroom and sprinted to make it in time. I really did think that one of my messages was going to be that I had to go home because I couldn't hold it any longer… Did I mention that the bathrooms were heated?

Nancy and I had a nice chat with the ranger who was outside the bathroom when I came out. After she asked what we were doing that day and we told her of our plan to snowshoe to Black Pond. She said to have a great time. I of course asked what her plans were, failing to notice her attire, which has 'park ranger' and trees embroidered on the sleeves and front of the shirt, and shiny bronze name plate. Both Nancy and the ranger answered, in unison, "working". We all laughed. Yup, that's me, always the observant one. So, I invite those that see me hosting an event, come along and if you are in need of a laugh and can't laugh at yourself, you're always free to laugh at me…

When we were all assembled in the parking lot and introductions to a new Hiking Buddy were made, we broke out in a series of colorful adjectives about the traffic, and I knew we were going to have a great day.

We started our trek with a stop at the ranger station for a before photo, and to make sure that the same number of people came out of the woods that had gone in. Then we were off. Across the suspension bridge, which some of us enjoyed more than others. Of course, I wanted to make it bounce and swing, but was out voted, so I satisfied myself with hopping across. Have you ever tried hopping in snowshoes? You'd think it would make it easier, I mean, look at rabbits with those ridiculously large back feet, but I assure you, I am no rabbit. The bouncing was fun, and I knew better than to try and take a picture while crossing, still reeling from dropping my phone in the port-a-potty this spring.

The reason I chose Lincoln Woods for Sunday's hike was because it was time to make peace with my arch nemesis. After last year's trip up to Owls Head, which left me 17 hours on my feet, and literally being dragged (at least emotionally) through Lincoln Woods, which seemed to NEVER END. Then after a ZBONDs traverse over the summer, where, again Lincoln Woods give you a false sense of the end, but you are not finished, you still have a stretch of flat land that seems to continue to multiply itself with every step.

We had some great views along the way. We talked and walked in silence and played leap frog with a photographer who was travelling on skis. Our trip down the snowy lanes felt enchanted and it was as if we'd stepped through our own magical wardrobe and straight into Narnia itself. The weather reports called for snow, but we were pleasantly surprised with a gift of sunlight. Once we reached the Black Pond Trail which was less broken out we took a little break to watch a small dog running towards us on the Lincoln Woods Trail, only to realize that the small dog was really a large rabbit, Narnia indeed, perhaps with a touch of Alice's Wonderland.

I selfishly broke trail so that I could see down the snowy lanes and we got to Black Pond in quicker than our normal turtle pace, while everyone tried to claim the coveted slowest speed hiker in the group. I think it ended up being a draw. After finding a good lunch spot, passing our friend the photographer, and snacking, we were on our way baack.

On the way back I found the perfect spot for our DAMNS hiking buddies photo op. As I worked diligently at setting up my phone atop a log and using my poles as a stand, which wasn't going as well as planned, and getting everyone organized, and stomping in the snow to get a quick passage to my correct location, and telling everyone to get into the wrong positions, and the phone still not getting perched very well, then when it finally seemed to be in a good spot, Stacy exclaimed "oh, I have a tripod!" about the time Nancy makes the statement "we should be able to this with an engineer, a lawyer, and two nurses on hand."

Stacy asks "who's the engineer?"

I answered, "that would be me, you know the one that couldn't figure out how to use the tripod, and apparently I can't spell either, since I tried to put everyone in DAMNS position and then proceeded to make Stacy stand next to Diane, and then put Michelle at the end, so much for retiring and wanting to be a writer..."

After we FINALLY got situated and got the DAMNS shot. I coerced everyone to sit along the trail to get something FUN for the Hiking Buddies page. I started the camera and jumped into my spot, only to have the back of my snowshoe drop into the snow and twist itself upside down taking my foot/leg/and twisting me into a rather unflattering position. To which all attention was diverted from the said camera, and as hard as I tried I couldn't turn myself, well, in any direction. Then we were all stuck! After the laughter subsided, we pulled and twisted and each managed to get back on our feet somehow. And though no one was looking at the camera, we decided to not try another shot as it took us longer to get back up than it did hiking out to the pond itself.

It is true that laughter is the best medicine! And a great way to add a spring to your step.

It worked! We had a blast! Peace has been made and only time will tell if it will last.

It was time to hike with my Lisa again. So grateful for all the new friends that I have made thanks to Hiking Buddies. Lisa got a chance to show off one of her favorite locations and I got to check off another 52WAV. The great Welch-Dickey Loop was the hike of the day.

Yes, I know that it's not all about The List(s), but sometimes it's just nice to have another one on the books.

I am in awe of the folks that post a write-up and pictures the same day they hike, sometime within the hour or even while on trail. While I usually take three days for a turn around a post hike post.

So, the following was written and posted the same day of the hike with a few tweaks having made since the original post.

First and foremost a HUGE shout out to Lisa for agreeing to join me. Love you lady!!!

We had an amazing time and superb weather. As per my moto, 'If the Whites are white, then snowshoes rule the day.' Yeah, it's a lame moto, but it's mine. :-D

I was supremely happy to have the extra surface area for stepping since there was indeed a set of bare boots on the trail either the day before or that morning. Yup, a Post-holer, mucked up the trail. Did what I could to even things out.

That just made the trek that much more interesting. Paying attention to the footsteps actually helped me see some snow fleas, which I was only aware of because Mike Cherim posted a picture just a couple of days before our outing. Not to worry, they are beneficial bugs that help in the breakdown of decaying matter, found often along the base of trees.

Fun Fact

Researchers at Queen's University in Canada have examined the anti-freeze protein that allows snow fleas to be active at colder temperatures. They believe that by better understanding these proteins, similar ones can be used to better store transplant organs and even make better ice cream!

I think I'll pass on the snow flea ice-cream, but hey, kudos Canada, I do love research.

As Steve Smith said when I stopped by The Mountain Wanderer on my way home. "Welch-Dickey, the biggest bang for the buck."

Indeed it was. Views, views, views, views. Once we hit the first overlook, we had literally views the whole way up to Welch Mountain, over and up to Dickey Mountain and all the way to the parking lot.

The forecast indicated mostly cloudy skies, but they held off until we were on our way out. We were blessed with a beautiful clear day and able to enjoy the endless vistas.

The following day I was signed up to join Sundar once again. Back to the Valley Way Trail, but this time he was attempting to summit Adams. I was willing to go the whole way with him if need be, because that's what Hiking Buddies is all about. Find our people and keep each other safe.

Yes, up in the mountains two days in a row. Another unbelievably beautiful day. I only did 3.5 miles with 1224 ft elevation gain. Since the day before was a 4.3 mile day with 1911 ft elevation gain, I'd say getting that much a second day out in the Whites wasn't too bad.

Before we started we got to visit with one of the favorite White Mountain's ambassadors. It's always fun to snap a shot with everyone's favorite Candyman. I did scold him a bit since it was only a few weeks since he broke his leg and was out hiking without giving himself the proper time to heal. I let him know that, "Eric, I do wish you'd give yourself some time to recover."

It was still good to see him out there and was glad that he was feeling better, but pretty sure you could use some actual time off that leg. Oops, did I write that out loud?

When a Hiking Buddy, especially a turtle, asks if you want to join in some elevation fun, you answer the call. Another great turnout! Thank you Sundar for hosting and fellow turtles, Laura, Cheryl and a new hiking buddy Sierra for coming forward so when I was feeling like I needed to turn back, there was still a good group to pick up the baton and sally forth. I was struggling a bit after hiking the day before, so after a while I snapped one more group shot and back down I went. I was hoping to making it to the hut, but just wasn't feeling it. I enjoyed just getting out there all the same.

Quiz time… Can anyone guess what I was wearing on my feet? Hint – The Whites are still covered in white.

Yes, Love me some snowshoe action. I was thinking of calling myself Snowshoe Jo. Or is giving myself a nickname (or trail name) unnecessary, since I'm pretty sure everyone knows where I stand on this issue? I was super stoked whenever I saw a fellow snowshoer though, and I started whoopin' and a hollerin'.

The Valley Way Trail is another stunner and I was happy to join my trailmates for that amazing day. We did discuss how I failed to post the Madison summit a few weeks before. Though it never made it as a post hike post on FB, it did earn a spot here in the book.

I enjoyed seeing my fellow turtles show off some stunning shots from Adams. After all the sun was still out as I wrote my post hike post.

MOOSILAUKE FINALLY

It had been about five years since I started hiking in the White Mountains and checking off 4000 Footers. Since then I had talked about, seen the infamous orange signs, even made up a little song about this elusive mountain. The little song was,

"Moosilauke

Moosilauke

Moosilauke."

OK, so it wasn't very imaginative or melodic, but my former hiking companions used to sing, or chant it with me whenever we got together. We would hike something else, sing our song and say, "next hike."

But something else would always come up. The weather wasn't favorable, someone else needed something else for their list, we just weren't feeling in, it was too close – we're only here for a couple days lets do something further away, etc. Then those relationships dissolved as they sometimes do. I was left to find others to hike with or strike out as a solo hiker.

So, during the pandemic, but after they re-opened the White Mountains, I took a trip up to New Hampshire. Goal was to do a solo hike at Mount Cardigan, then following day hit Moosilauke. Well, Cardigan was summited, but it wasn't pretty and I didn't have my Garmin Mini2 yet, and though I sent messages before and after to loved ones, I scared myself so much that I opted to come back another day.

Two and a half years after the solo "attempt," though I'm not sure you can call it an attempt if you never even made it to the trailhead, I kept up the "let's do Moosilauke" planning.

I even hosted a Hiking Buddies event, where most of the crew did summit. I, personally made it to about a half mile or so from the summit and decided that I wasn't feeling it, so thankfully had one of the buddies turn back with me. Then another non-attempt, even though we were at the trailhead, we decided to hike Blueberry Mountain instead. I highly recommend Blueberry Mountain if someone is looking for a great hike.

Jennifer reached out, knowing that I was pining to hike Moose, and offering to help me out. The almost always willing Nancy joined in on the adventure. Some of my other buddies wanted to join but were unable to attend. Jennifer, Nancy, and I made our plan to try yet again. The weather looked better and better as the time approached, so it was a definite go. After much discussion and intel from Steve Smith, we decided to try the Gorge Brook/Carriage Road/Snapper Trail loop.

Getting there, no matter how you slice it, or where you come from, a trip on NH-118 is required. Only a week earlier I drove from Lincoln to Glencliff trailhead, about 13 miles on 118. There was a sign stuck in the snow at the beginning of the road that read FROST HEAVES. I had no idea what that even meant and then thought, well, how bad could it be. No sooner did I have that thought then the waves began. Up and down, and up and down, then every once in a while a piece of road was broken and you had to swerve to stop from dropping into a hole, mostly it was just up and down. Kind of like being in a rowboat on Lake Michigan in October. It can be done, but it's not recommended. Here we were a week later and thankfully, only 7ish miles on said frosty heavy road, but this time there are also signs that warn BUMP. As Jennifer stated, "what was that then?"

Sure enough, the frost heaves in just a week had gotten even more pronounced and the BUMPS meant, "these sections can send you airborne or rip out the undercarriage, or better yet cause you to end up in a crater. So, we went from the rowboat effect to straight up a rollercoaster ride at your favorite amusement park. Good thing vehicles come equipped with their own seatbelts. Once again I was fighting motion sickness before reaching the parking lot. Off of 118 and onto Ravine Road, which I was concerned about since reports of cars sliding off because it was icy, prior to the additional snow we received. Luckily, Ravine Road going in was pretty good, packed snow for the most part with dirt peeking through the center of the road made it fairly easy to navigate up to the second gate and parking area.

I was the first one in the parking area. Plenty of time to eat my bagel, change into my hiking boots, put on the gaiters, get myself sorted. As the rest of the team arrived I was hoping to just slap on my snowshoes, then I see that we have an actual road walk up to the trailhead. Instead my snowshoes will have to get attached to the pack and I put my microspikes on instead. This makes me grumpy, and childlike, so after pulling the microspikes out of my pack I slam the back door. I intended sitting in the front seat to put on the spikes. As soon as the door closes I hear the clickity click of all the doors locking, yes, with my keys stowed safely in my backpack, which is sitting on the back seat.

Good news, I have my phone so I can call AAA. Bad news, no signal. Maybe 911? As I was whining and complaining and ready to hoof it down the road until I got a signal, a good Samaritan parked next to Nancy offered to help. Lo and behold he had the tools and skillset to pop open the door within minutes. He totally saved the day! Thank you kind stranger. That's what I get for throwing a tantrum before we even get started. Hopefully I learned my lesson and let cooler heads prevail when I unwittingly don't get my own way.

After an exciting start to the day and because we showed up early and found a helpful soul, we were only five minutes behind our original start time.

The 0.8 mile road walk to the trailhead was fairly uneventful, except noting that it was going to be a climb back up to the parking lot and we contemplated taking the hiking trail back, since that looked like it stayed at the same level as the lot. Because the last thing you want to do at the end of a long day is finish on an uphill. There's a beautiful lodge at the end of the road. My favorite observation about the lodge area was an outhouse with a padlock. It just made me chuckle and then I had to look for a pee tree.

There is a bridge that takes you to the trailhead. The day we crossed it there was a couple feet of snow on it and plenty of post holes which made it even more narrow. It was like crossing a balance beam of snow. Yes, we didn't help the situation, since we put our snowshoes on after we crossed.

I did get some excellent shots of Nancy's backpack putting on technique. She swings that bad boy up over her head. It is an amazing sight. I tried it once, but ended up almost knocking myself out as the bag swung uncontrollably and banged the side of my skull. I'll stick to the one shoulder in then shimmy and untwist method.

I'm always grateful for snowshoes on a snowy trail, even if it's packed out. We marched along in mostly silence, since the crunching from the snowshoes usually makes conversation just a bit harder to manage. We ascended in silence for the most part, which is a blessing or a curse depending on what mood the committee (yes, all those voices in my head) is in. Mostly, while hiking it's great, and my best lines come to me, of course by the time I get to write them down they are long gone. So, my best work is usually stolen from Nancy. As we started on the trail, I stated that "third time is a charm."

However, the second time we didn't even step onto the trail, so I was told that didn't count. Even though I DID take the wavy road trip to the Glencliff trailhead, the day we decided to hike Blueberry Mountain instead.

Let it be known that this was the very first hike with the incredible Nancy that I was not slowing her down. Yes, I was being spoiled and getting in more hikes than ever. Jennifer saved the day when she suggested we take a snack break since we all didn't realize how much we needed it.

We were in no hurry and stepping aside for others gave us our rest pit breaks. Jennifer was also the one to remind us to look up and we had the most incredible views as we basked in the sun and there was much ooing and ahhing.

We couldn't have asked for a prettier day. The rest of the way to the summit was a pleasant stroll with plenty of breaks to just enjoy the scenery. We added the layers ditched early on as we hit the alpine zone. The sun made it feel much warmer than it actually was, so as we broke through the trees the whiteness of the summit gave great contrast to the colorful figures in the distance. Those are the times that it feels other worldly when looking at everything covered in rime ice. It felt as if we'd stepped off the Enterprise and half expecting an alien with lavender skin or perhaps a third eye to greet us along the way.

And though I know it is nothing like Everest, I can almost imagine how someone could want to make that a quest. The cold, quiet, starkness of it all just seems to help you breath deeper and clearer.

We took it nice and slow going up to the summit. Finally, I got to see the notable orange summit sign and incredible 360 degree views. We were amazed at the ski mountaineers. Those are some bad asses. Actually skiing UP the mountain. Damn, it's hard enough walking.

Nancy asked if anyone had come up Snapper Trail. One of the skiers answered that they had and stated that "we'd appreciate it if you wear snowshoes."

Yes!

We decided on the loop and took the carriage road back down, waiting to lunch out of the wind. We found a nice little nestled spot to drop ourselves and our packs and hoped we were off trail enough to not get run over by any skiers on their way back down. But also didn't want to go off trail and get caught in a spruce trap, from the looks of it the snow was definitely deep enough to be over your head in some places.

When we started back down, we saw the sign saying "You are on the carriage Road Trail" so knew we were heading in the right direction. We got to the junction that connected the Carraige Road, Snapper Trail, South Peak and Glencliff Trail. We all passed on South Peak, yes, I did manage to get to it last time, but with no views. Yes, I was ok with not getting views that day. So, off to Snapper Trail we wandered. Only to find it a post holing nightmare. I swear that it almost obliterated the good time right out of my head. And yes, swear is what I did. I think about half way down I literally stopped, raised my little fists with my poles over my head, and let out a primordial yell "F%$& you Post-holers!!!!"

Hopefully, it's still reverberating today. And I implore you, if you're hiking in the snow, please wear snowshoes. Heck, it's right in the name...

Poor Nancy had been struggling with an Achilles issue. After I yelled, Nancy agreed that, "Going downhill is a lot more difficult than it should be."

We finally made it to the Gorge Brook Trail to take us back to the Lodge. Finally, relief, a nicely packed trail never felt so good. Once crossing back over the bridge, which was even more like crossing a balance beam of snow, with a mis-step landing you in the frozen brook, we discussed whether we should take the trail back to the parking lot, or continue on the road from whence we came. I have never once heard Nancy complain before but she even stated. "I can't take one more twist or turn. Post-holers!"

It was decided, road it is, even if we have to go uphill, at least it's solid.

Then the next question left to ask was "what's the next adventure?"

CRAZY OR BEGINNING OF A GRID?

I hiked Owl's Head once again. How, you may be wondering, did that happen? Life is a many splendor thing and opportunities to do things we can't always imagine sometimes present themselves at the strangest times and in an unplanned way. My second time doing this mighty hike happened again in the winter and was done as a mostly solo hike.

Yes, even after the previous February's longest day. That was 17 hours on my feet with the concluding "Thank God That's Over" statement. Why, oh why, would I feel the need to ever do that hike again? Especially when I have so many yet unhiked hikes awaiting me?

I was intrigued and felt the desire to get in on helping Tom achieve his Over 70 - 48 Single Season (why winter, only Tom can answer that) goal. It just looked like such a fun group. Hawaiian shirts, Tom and his unsmoked cigar, the enthusiastic fans, and the fact that Mike The-Man-with-a-Plan was leading the coordination charge all played a role in my interest.

Mike was one of those FB friends that I had yet to meet in person. I loved his writings, posts, attitude, and pretty much agreed with all comments to questions. I find myself saying "couldn't have said it better myself."

Yes, of course, then I would go ahead and give my opinion anyways.

I don't think Mike realized what it meant to me when he reached out to welcome me to New Hampshire. There I was hiking, writing, and basically upended my life as I knew it and took a leap of faith without knowing where or how I was going to land. The reason I'm writing this is to thank people like Mike. Mike had sent me a message welcoming me and shared a little of his similar journey. The inspiration of seeing someone else take that leap and land so gracefully then reach out a hand to help the next person succeed meant a lot to me.

While I don't know that I'll ever win any Pulitzers, I do hope that I can have one person relate to what I went through and perhaps give them someone to identify with. To help you take that step into the unknown and just believe. For I am remarkably unremarkable or remarkably ordinary, and I did it, and so can you.

Back to how "it" happened. Tom was down to his last three and a week to go with a snowstorm looming.

How the hell did that happen? You may be wondering. I think I'm still wondering the same thing myself. The long and short of it is, the hiking community is just awesome, and I enjoy being part of that awesomeness.

After reading Mike's posts about Tom and his quest to get his over 70 Single Season Winter (SSW) 48 – 4000 Footers goal complete with a week left to go and a snowstorm a brewing. My desire to be part of the solution caused me to reached out to Mike to offer my help in any way I could. I love tromping through the snow in my snowshoes so I sent a private message to Mike, just letting him know I was serious about my offer.

He let me know that they had a good crew for Isolation but would add me to the Owl's Head effort. Of course, I groaned to myself. One because I still hadn't hiked Isolation and it would have been nice to just tag along there. Two because, do I even really need to say it? It was Owl's Head. The LONGEST Day of my life. I think my feet still aren't right. After all, I had JUST come to some semblance of peace with Lincoln Woods.

There was talk of going out on Wednesday, but they decided that Friday would be the Owl's Head day. With another foot or so of snow dumped on Wednesday, my intention was to go out Thursday and break trail as far as I could. Then I received a report that a couple of folks were headed out to do just that. So, I switched to heading out early on Friday, knowing that I would be slower than the rest and didn't want to slow anyone down. I got there early enough to be on the trail an hour early. I had intended on sending out a message, but no signal, so I just headed out.

The trail breakers did an excellent job and I just cruised right along. I was about seven miles in when I decided to take a little break. Lesson learned from last year. Get off my feet, if only for a few minutes from time to time. And I figured that Team Tom would be catching up at that point. As I was having a snack, a couple trail runners passed me by, I asked if they had seen the Hawaiian party, they said no, but they came another way??? I still have no idea what that meant. But they passed by and I didn't notice at first that they were bare booting it. Which means they were chewing up the trail, leaving divots, which I did my best to smooth over. Then another trail runner came by. She did have snowshoes and I was grateful that she did a sweep before I did.

I had given myself two turnaround times. The first was noon, if the group caught up to me, knowing I wouldn't be able to maintain their pace. The second was a summit time of 2pm. That way, maybe I could actually join the group for a while. I reached the Brutus Bushwack right around noon and started my ascent. The bushwack is THE steep section of the winter trail, this is where ALL of the elevation happens, OK only half of it. In about a mile section there's an elevation gain of approximately 1500 ft, which is half of the overall gain over an 8.5 mile trek to the summit.

What a difference a year makes. With it comes a whole lot of knowledge gained. Like having the right equipment. I purchased new snowshoes right after last year's LONGEST DAY, and they were my bestest friend that winter (sorry Nancy).

I even used my televators up that section of trail. I followed Nancy's lead from the Moosilauke trip and did 10 steps then take a break. Sometime a few more and sometimes a few less, but upward slowly and steadily. Everything is relative, so even though I guess it still goes up the last mile, it feels flat after the mile of straight up. So, reaching the "flat" area with a mile to go, it still wasn't 2pm, so onward I continued.

I cruised along as best I could, though even though it was flat, or seemingly so, it was more chewed up the closer to the summit. So, I cursed the bare booters, but before I knew it, I came through the familiar opening to the summit, which is never fully exposed, but very much burned in my memory that this was the end of the line and the top of Owl's Head. I looked at the time and what do you know? It was exactly 2:00 pm, my turnaround time.

I came back down the trail a bit and found a place to set up my pad in order to sit and have some lunch. I had intended to eat and change my socks and possibly take a little nap. As soon as I plopped into my open pad the colorful squad of Team Tom supporters did appear.

The first group was led by Mike with his Red jacket that matched by his rosy cheeks and bright smile. Finding a lone woman on a pad to greet them all, must have been quite the sight. Honestly, I was surprised at the sight myself. And as much as I wanted to get up and greet the troops, I was just pooped and not inclined to rise quite yet. I'd literally just plopped my pooped bod down after foraging my bag for food and additional layers.

I was super excited to see them all come through, even if it didn't seem so to the others. Plus, I wanted to give everyone space at the summit clearing, since it's not really that big. But I became a bit anxious when the first set of hikers arrived and then there was that awkward silence. So, I asked "where's Tom?" Hoping that I hadn't missed him somehow, and it seemed like such a loooong time that the first group emerged.

"He's coming," Mike answered. I'm pretty sure there were introductions as we waited, me still on my pad. As we continued to chat and Mike discovered that this was my second time up Owl's Head he exclaimed, "well now you're working on your Grid."

I can neither confirm nor deny that I have any intention of becoming a Gridiot. A Gridiot is the affection term that other hikers use for those that hike all 48 peaks in every month. This is that next level of crazy. I may be content with being only Two Owl's Head insane.

Then the second group came with Tom somewhere near the end. Of course, I rose to my feet because I had also brought a little something. Introduced myself and gave Tom a lei as he approached.

Yes, I summited Owl's Head for a second time, just so I could claim the very bad pun of "Abbie leied Tom on the Owl's Head."

Selfishly, I think I got the better part of the deal and met a whole new set of friends and colorful cast of characters. I used bad trail etiquette and put on new socks, while everyone waited on the trail. From there, I did let them know it was OK to leave me behind, since I had my Garmin activated and soloed up in the first place. I did stay with them up until we hit the Black Pond Trail, so with 5ish miles to go, I stated that they should not wait if I was to fall behind again, because I knew I'd take one more "off my feet break."

As soon as we approached Black Pond, I decided to take that last break and told the group to go ahead. I did get off my feet one last time and thanks to having my peace with Lincoln Woods knew I could manage that last four miles with ease.

I made sure I got the headlamp out and on my head as I got up to head on out. I was skipping along and all went well for a couple miles, then the rain started. With only a couple miles to go I didn't mind the precipitation and got to see how well my new rain jacket would hold up.

The darkness settled in with only a mile to go. That's when my mind started playing tricks with me of course. All of a sudden the sign that warned of bear activity from last fall flashed in my mind. It was there at the end of Lincoln Woods on our way out of the ZBONDs trip. Even though we were still in winter, all I could think with the warm rain falling that "tonight's the night that the bears are going to wake up and they are going to be HANGRY!"

I mean, I know how I get when my blood sugar level crashes. After several months of not eating I can only imagine how much worse a bear would feel.

Then of course, every shadow seemed to move and every noise was amplified. I would see paw prints in the snow with tracks going in and out of the woods. Asking myself "dog or bear prints?"

Obviously, they were dogs because all of them could be seen going to and fro. So, after running through the scenario where the very hungry bear smells the remnants of my PB&J and the handful of trail mix still in my backpack. The very hangry bear would know that there was food in its grasp. I'd feel the tug at my pack and I'd unclip and free myself letting the oversized form of fur, claws and teeth have at it.

Only then did I laugh at myself, and maybe quickened my step a bit. I started singing silly songs to myself and would target my next tree then tell myself, "just go that far while singing your song," and not thinking about the very hungry bear. It worked. So, another tree in the next hundred feet or so and sing another song.

This is the blessing and the curse of an over active imagination. I could think of things to distract myself from my "wake up bear scenario." But that visual of the bear was ever present.

FINALLY, in the distance, I saw the bridge to safety was shimmering ahead and I could breathe freely. As I crossed the bridge I saw bobbing lights knowing there were others above near the ranger station and what tension I still held finally released. Around the last bend and into the parking lot. I passed a couple of people with headlamps at a vehicle. They called out hello, and I answered with a "hey" and that to me is how we do.

I let the group know that I was on my way home when I got back on the road since I never have service in the Lincoln Woods parking lot. Only a few feet down the road I was able to pull over and send out a quick message. I was pleasantly surprised that one of the women, Beth, had answered saying that they'd waited for a while in the parking lot and the father and son who had said hello to me, she'd put on alert to keep an eye out.

Come to find out I was only a half hour behind the group, so if I'd continued inside of having my last break I'm sure I would have kept up with them. And I had seen Beth driving out of the lot as I was passing the ranger station.

All in all, my effort secured my spot on Tom's final hike, Mount Carrigan, a couple days later. I, however grateful for the invite, decided to decline the hike because it was too cold and windy and I needed more recovery time. I did go and meet them at the afterparty.

ANOTHER NOT FINAL FINISH

I took a couple days to recover from Owl's Head, then I reached out to a couple of hiking buddies to tackle another mountain that I didn't want to leave for my last. I figured it would be the last really good day to take advantage of the winter bushwack to Mount Isolation. Nancy and Cheryl were up for the task so away we went.

I think we may have had the final best winter weather and perfect trail conditions of the season. OK, technically spring had sprung but the winter bushwack was well established and conditions were predicted to be cold enough to keep things from completely falling apart.

This was on my list of "don't leave to be your final," so after Michele and I had bailed over the summer and conditions were as they were I decided to give it a go.

The planning was most important on this one. Definitely not one that I felt comfortable going solo. I think we rescheduled three or four times over the winter. Unfortunately our core crew couldn't all make it, and I was sad that Michele couldn't join us since she's the one that asked me what my thoughts were on hiking that day. She ended up having to work. I keep telling folks that work is the worst of the four letter words. Of course I will do it again when she's available, but it was time to make haste with the little bit of solid winter weather available.

Christine and Stacy also had to work. That left Nancy and I. Then I heard from someone I'd met at the Wilderness Presentation and her and her husband said they were in. I got an invite by someone to do something in the Belknaps, but I turned the invite around and it was a potential that she'd join us. Thursday night the couple called out, saying they were going on Wednesday instead. I heard that another group got canceled for Wednesday, so Cheryl had reached out because she was in the Wednesday group so I asked her to join us.

We ended up with three, which turned out to be the perfect number. The trail conditions were perfect heading out. Of course I wore my snowshoes the whole time, even though it wasn't necessarily necessary. The feeling of spring was in the air and it was a good trek up. Snow bridges in tact and the crunchy cold snow that just feels good under foot. The question was, how was the river crossing going to be? Rumors had it that it was sketchy soon after the bushwhack was established.

We got there and the water was shallow and rocks exposed. Sweet!

Nancy transitioned to snowshoes for the last half mile or so to the summit, which was pretty much straight upness. The summit was stellar. Clear views of Washington, there was a bit of a wind, and yes it was chilly. We got some great shots of George (Mount Washington that is, I figured we were on a first name basis by now since I had relocated for him after all) just as the clouds decided to start obscuring him. After summit lunch we headed back down. I stayed in my snowshoes while Nancy transitioned back to her super microspikes. Cheryl had stayed in her microspikes the whole time.

On the way up we were passed by a solo woman, solo man, and a couple couples (not to imply that they were a couple in the sense of romantically inclined, but rather meaning they were with other individuals.)

While you may have heard of Capt. Obvious, you may refer to me as Madame Oblivious. Congratulations to the woman who was wearing the tiara who had completed her 48 on Isolation that day. She gave us a heads up that the other solo hiker also finished his, so I at least I got to congratulate one of them.

On our way down there was way too much up to be going down. How is it that Rocky Branch Trail feels like you're going up both ways? As I had anticipated the snow began to mush up near the end of the day and we had more than a couple of the snow bridges fall apart under our feet.

Timing is a many splendored thing, and our timing was perfect that day! Thank you for the snow and the heavenly trail breaker outers. Your efforts were much appreciated.

Special thanks to my companions for another successful peak bagging episode. With honorable mention to Nancy for leading the songs, which I can never remember the words, but I sing harmony as best as I can.

BEST LAID PLANS TURN INTO ADVENTURE EXPLORING

I met up with Samia for this one. Our initial plan was to hike up Mount Washington via Ammonoosuc Trail, which I'd hoped to snag Monroe as well before heading over to the big guy and coming down Jewell.

The weather did not cooperate, so we changed our plans. Samia suggested Mount Livermore (not a 4000 Footer or 52WAV but part of the White Mountain Guide), but she'd already gone up Cotton Mountain and over, so we decided on another route. We planned on starting up Brooks Fisher Trail and over to Livermore.

I was feeling like a baby and not looking forward to the drive, since it would be an hour and a halfish. When I hit the dirt road that lasted for the last 4 miles or so, I was even more of a baby. It was slicker than snot and the old slide factor was in effect. Even though I left home early, I ended up getting to the trailhead just at our agreed to start time.

Even though I was pouty to start, here's something about actually hiking that puts everything right. We started out fairly good with I in my snowshoes, and Samia as well. This made for easy work to what we thought was a water crossing. I followed her pup Zhetti, like spaghetti, and I popped over the stream. Actually Zhetti was in the stream getting a drink. I was just following a set of tracks, or so I thought, but then nothing. Oh, the trail didn't cross, so we went back across the stream and followed the red blazes. Came across an old headstone. We couldn't really read it because it was so old but what an enchanting find. As we were talking about it I noticed a bright blue something ahead, was it a tent? No, a car, not just any car, my car. Yup, we were back at the parking lot. Madame Oblivious strikes again. I still can't believe that really I didn't even realize that I was taking us back from where we came. Thankfully it was only a few hundred feet and Lord help all that follow me.

Back on track and to the end of the trail where we found a nice spot to overlook the lake while enjoying lunch. The hope was to knock out another section of trail by going out and back an additional 1.4 miles. Except to get there we had to follow tracks of a damn postholer, literally one dude up to probably his knee the whole way. Who does that?

Sorry to say that after the mile of following the postholer tracks, I was not up for the additional out and back, so we headed to the road to make our loop for the day. And the life of a White Mountain Guide tracer is that I will surely be back to get that section we didn't take time for and more.

FRANCONIA RIDGE

What to say about hiking the infamous Franconia Ridge? All of the feelings from excitement to trepidation, and from despair to elation. They were all there. I feel like this was the hardest hike I've ever done. Not only physically but emotionally as well. I had been enthralled by the Franconia Ridge for quite a while, ever since I read Ty Gagne's book *The Last Traverse* and heard Ty's own story about struggling on the ridge.

I was waiting for the right day to be fully prepared before taking on the challenge. The tragedy of Emily Sotelo still weighs heavy in my heart. I have simultaneously been inspired by the many who have shared their experiences in photos and stories of the beauty and the wonder that the ridge offers those bold enough to explore. I believe Franconia Ridge and Mount Washington are the most hiked areas in the Whites. If not the most hiked, they are the most notorious.

About a week before the hike I had been looking at the forecasts and thought perhaps my chance to hike up Mount Washington might be realized. Before I could get too far into the planning I heard from one of my hiking buddies that he was going to plan on tackling Franconia Ridge that same day. With the weather looking promising and my desire strong I was happy to say yes. So, thanks to Sundar for setting up this amazing Hiking Buddies expedition. There were nine of us total including Nancy, Laurie, Eugenia, Beth, Paul and Tran.

Our group gathered in the parking lot and we all suited up. It's always interesting to discover what the dynamics of a group of people is going to be. I had hiked with most of the people before. A year earlier, Eugenia and I had actually joined Stacy's buddy hike up Lafayette, so to be able to hike with Eugenia again was a true pleasure.

Everyone chose footwear with various forms of traction. Mine included a landing pad around my traction, you caught me, yes, my snowshoes. It was just a habit at that point I suppose.

The thing with a larger group like we had was that changing plans based on conditions wasn't an easy thing to do. Knowing the forecast was indicating that winds would pick up early afternoon and us starting at 8:30, I figured we'd hit Lafayette right about the time things started going downhill weather wise. Part of me wanted to reach out and ask if we could start at 5:00 am, but most everyone had a commute and I was just going along for the ride so to speak. I do know that if the windspeeds looked any higher than what was projected, I would have bailed and attempted another day. Plus, it was supposed to be cold up there, which was hard to imagine with temps at the trailhead nearing 40, but I believed the forecast and was very prepared.

Nancy was the first in the parking lot and by her own admission would probably be the last one ready.

Feeling like I was definitely ready. Hadn't I just successfully taken on Owl's Head, Moosilauke, and Isolation recently and felt all the stronger for achieving those accomplishments?

Many thoughts about *The Last Traverse* played through my mind. I could hear the wind, blowing up on the ridge, from the parking lot, at least I thought I could, though I know it didn't start for us until we were up on the ridge. I feel like we were being looked after even as the conditions began to deteriorate, but I'm jumping ahead.

We started on time and I enjoyed seeing some of the falling water along the Falling Waters Trail. I was surprised at how quickly I began to labor. Just for me, this ended up being the most difficult hike I recalled doing to that date. Mind you my first Owl's Head was definitely the longest, but I really dragged up the Falling Waters Trail. I brought up the rear or should I say I was dragging my rear in the rear.

I was back to my usual holding Nancy back pace. The beauty of the trail, patience of the group, and conversations of others helped to keep me motivated up to the Little Haystack approach. That was the time that Nancy had decided to turn back. Though I hated to see her go, I'm glad she did what was right for her. I was tempted to return with her but I also felt a second wind at that point and was eager to behold the wonders of the ridge.

My energy level began to rise after we stopped to eat and add a layers before emerging on the alpine zone. I was thankful to take the lead for the last little bit to the summit of Little Haystack. There was something about having the good vibes from the group feeling like they were pushing me from behind.

We all quickly layered up as soon as we reached Little Haystack. I imagine what deep sea divers must go through before braving the waters of the Arctic cold. If nothing else, I was indeed warm and then ready to forge ahead. It was about 20 degrees colder than at the trailhead. There was some blue sky then and little to no wind to speak of yet. I was famished even though we'd just stopped for food right before our last push to the ridge.

Then, I got to see ridge up close and personal. I also felt it with all my being. It was like seeing the Christmas tree standing in the living room just waiting to bring joy after Santa's visit. How exciting and peaceful at the same time. We started ahead and I knew there was no turning back now. We made good time getting to the rocky outcrop about half way to Lincoln when we could feel the weather start turning. On to Lincoln, as we started going up was when I felt my energy drain from me. The wind let its presence be known. Even though I was warm and comfortable in my layers, the struggle for me began. I fell way behind the group and was starving once more.

There is something about reaching a summit that you work hard for that makes it that much more satisfying and this was one of those times. It began snowing and the smokey swirls of loose snow painted the way with a picturesque warning. The sun would try and break through as Lafayette was calling us onward.

After eating again I had not adhere my face covering correctly and as we started the ascent to Lafayette the wind did start in earnest. By then my face covering was all but off and my pants had started to slip down. I started to sing the "Pants on the Ground" song. Sometimes you just have to motivate yourself, between the wind and my snowshoes crunching and scraping no one could really hear me anyways. Thankfully Laurie did ask how I was doing and noticed my face covering hanging precariously, it was not really doing me any good at that point. I answered that I was struggling and she went into Mom mode to help get me put back together.

We continued on and though I was now composed, so to speak, I still had to reach deep to get to the summit of Lafayette. That same feeling as when I was giving birth hit me "I can't do this." But, we were too far along to worry about that now. Just one foot in front of the other. At this time Sundar was now pulling up the rear and I was so grateful to see the rest of the team around the summit sign. A few photos at the top and then it's all downhill from here, well, not quite.

Getting off of Lafayette can pose its own challenge and this is where many have gone astray. A couple steps heading down and I was going ass over teakettle. Nothing hurt, but unable to see my footing was now at play and once again I was going slowly but surely. Beth initially went forward and made it to maybe the second cairn when we had no idea where to go from there. My hands were too cold from just getting a drink of water and looking at the map initially to see if we were on track. Tran Le stopped up, and helped navigate us off of the mountain.

Another group of three, whom we'd seen in the distance for quite a while, passed by us as we waited for all of our group to gather together again. The spruce patch was just in front of us and we could see that Greenleaf Hut was not too far away. Paul asked if I needed a rest and I knew that the hut would be the perfect place to do that so I said I'd prefer to press onward.

The trip through the spruce trees is always enchanting, even if at that time of the year they feel a little grabby on the backpack. It always amazes me how far away the hut looks when you first enter and in moments it feels like it magically appears in front of you. Some sanctuary before heading down. The relief and sense of awe began to fill me again. We did it! It was amazing and scary and hard but we did it!

The year before, with Stacy's Lafayette group, we dubbed a spot on the far side of the hut as the most scenic bathroom in the Whites. After a brief rest I took a visit to the most scenic bathroom and we were on our way back down. With all the face coverings no longer needed, a layer or two or three could be removed. I could see my feet once more and had the distinguished honor of leading the way.

Only one bum touch, that's where your butt hits the ground, and we made a hasty retreat, well until we got to one of the more spectacular viewing locations of the ridge.

It was even more amazing because we got to say "OMG can you believe that we just did that?" It looked so incredibly majestic and we all took some time to just be in awe. More layers came off and only one more stop on the way down because for some reason that last mile is always the longest.

It is absurd to me how much I enjoy hearing the sounds of the cars on the road as we were approaching the finish. Counter intuitive after working so hard to get out do what I so love to do.

Thanks again to everyone that made this a most memorable occasion. And Hiking Buddies for bringing us all together.

AN ACCIDENT, A NO GO, SOME RE-DOS, WATCH YOUR GPS

It was the last day of March and I was finally headed to hike Mount Major. That is a mountain too small to be considered for the 52WAV list but very notable and has been on my radar to hike because of its supposedly spectacular views of Lake Winnipesaukee. A hiking buddy that I had yet had the pleasure of meeting was to join me.

I headed out bright and early so I could stop along the way and grab a little breakfast to have at the trailhead. The whole figuring out when and what to eat thing is still an ongoing process. With a two hour drive to the trailhead I decided getting something close to the trailhead was in order. I left early enough, picked up some breakfast at a Dunkin Donuts along the way. I continued on and my GPS was slow on verbalizing directions that morning and failed to inform me that my turn was coming up. I saw the trailhead parking lot sign whiz by me as DESIREE piped in, "location on left."

I didn't know how long it would be before I could find somewhere to safely pull off the road and turn around. Seeing a break in the traffic headed towards me, I made the unwise choice to try and pull a U-Turn right then and there. I put on my left turn signal and swung the car a little right, then hard left. But, alas, the car behind me had caught up and was trying to pass, which I failed to realize that he had closed the gap. And that, my friends is how the front end of my car became totaled, though not in the eyes of the insurance company. And I ended up in the Laconia Hospital. The hospital staff did a wonderful job making sure that I was not badly injured. I was just a bit banged up a bit.

My new hiking buddy was able to hike up the mountain and down again. She called around and found out what hospital I was in and even brought me a coffee. She showed up just as I was being released and graciously brought me to the garage where my car was. Just another example of why I love the wonderful hiking community.

Mount Major would have to wait and I would have the pleasure of going around and around with insurance, find a body shop and, have to decide whether to repair the vehicle or take the money and run. I chose to have it repaired. A few months of using a rental vehicle and I was back in business.

Early April was upon us when Nancy and I decided it was time to hike up Kearsarge North. We wanted to spend the night in the fire tower, which is a first come first serve situation. We had been talking about doing this all winter, but every time Nancy suggested that we go, the temperatures plummeted into the very negative numbers. I was the weak link and said I was not prepared or willing to sleep outside (yes, technically it's inside, but only in the fact that you are out of the elements, not out of the cold) in those conditions.

Finally, it was supposed to be just below freezing and not a weekend, because I also didn't want to fight the crowds that were now beginning to make their way to the mountains as weekend warriors. We set the date.

We met early enough in the afternoon to get to the summit before sunset so we could still set up our sleeping quarters with some natural light. As we started our ascent you could feel spring trying to make itself present. And as I would come to find out, that means, lots of water flowing and plenty of mud along with the sound of birds making their way back up North after their retreat to warmer weather.

With the birds singing and a sloggy beginning we were hopeful. As it was "spring" in the Whites we were also prepared with our traction. And about a mile in, the trail had a fair amount of ice cover with a sheen from the wet, warmer water as it was actively melting. This made conditions okay as we were going up, but we quickly realized it was more icy the further we went. Knowing that the temperatures were due to drop overnight we made the decision to abandon the "Princess Project."

I called it the Princess Project because we were to spend the night in a tower, like a princess in the stories we grew up with.

We had made it about a mile when we decided to turn back. There were no regrets because we knew that as much as we wanted the experience, we knew the tower and the mountain would still be there and we would try again.

A few days later, Nancy and I would join Stacy's event for Mount Cardigan. Ah, Cardigan, whom I've held ill will towards since October 17, 2020. My first solo hike, which scared the crap out of me enough to get active with Hiking Buddies and not put myself in peril again.

All the way up I kept saying, "I think I took the right here."

Even at places where there wasn't a trail. In my tales I had stated that I had spent 0.5 mi going up a steep open ridge where I wanted to sit, cry, and blow my whistle. This memory is better described in the chapter "FIRST SOLO HIKE IN THE WHITES".

It was a lovely spring day, with a little mud, mashed potatoes, monorail, a few icy spots, and good ole bare rock on open ledges near the summit. Luckily it was cold enough that there was no post holing, though we could see where others had post holed previously. Must have gone all the way up to their crotch, and not in a good way. For the first time since probably November, my snowshoes got to take a ride instead of getting abused.

Mount Cardigan went from being a place of fear to turning into one of my very favorite. While we were at the summit and decided to check out going down the way I had come up on my solo hike. Lo and behold as we peered down the steep ledge, there was some ice down below and we all agreed that it looked treacherous indeed and that my fear from that solo day were not unfounded and we decided to go down the trail we had taken up.

Since we were still riding on our high from the Mount Cardigan experience Nancy and I decided to take a run at Madison. Nancy still needed Madison for her second round of the 48s.

We made it to about a mile from the hut on Valley Way. Decided that neither of us really had the legs to continue. The most important thing is that we return in one piece.

We went up in our spikes, well Nancy had her new K-10s which were a much better option than my microspikes. At the time we decided to turn around, I opted for my snowshoes.

On the way down we decided to take all the side trails to see the waterfalls. It was the perfect decision. Nancy opted to put on her snowshoes for the side trails. We decided that waterfalls were the theme for that day's hike.

Another unsummitted mountain with no regrets.

Remember Mount Major? Here we were, exactly two weeks after the accident trying to get there to hike, and it was time to give it another shot. This time I was going to hike with Nancy. At one point

Nancy said, "a lot of people get taken off this mountain in a litter." I said "Some get taken in a litter at the base of the mountain." Yes, referring to getting taken to the hospital after my accident.

We took the blue trail up which had a small section of icy stuff. It actually split there and you could go to the right (Nancy and I did) with microspikes and just breeze up the ice. Or up the left side and kind of work your way around the icy stuff, which is what we saw EVERYBODY else do. Well, except for the one guy who slid down the rocky ledge, I'm pretty sure he slid right into a tree. Now when they say bushwhack, I'm pretty sure they don't mean to take on a full body blow and let the bush (or tree for that matter) whack you.

I hadn't transitioned to my lighter pack yet, but took out things like my puffy, fleece, and extra socks, hat, and neck gaiter. So, one woman commented on "oh my, what a pack."

Personally, I think she was suffering from backpack envy. :-D

Nancy and I ended up having a picture perfect day and plenty of the amazing views that I've heard so much about. So, I must ask Ken why Mount Major isn't one of the 52WAVs?

A week later a few of my tried and true hiking buddies joined me for a Black Mountain in Benton adventure. Though I knew everyone, it was the first time the other ladies would be meeting each other.

New friendships were forged in the magic of the mountains.

We were planning on doing a traverse by going up the Chippewa Trail and down the Black Mountain Trail. So I suggested that we all meet at the Black Mountain trailhead, where we'd be finishing.

Sign, sign, everywhere a sign, as Lisa would find out. Unfortunately, her GPS sent her onto a private road off of Lime Kiln Road. This happened to be on the Chippewa Trailhead side of the mountain. After passing some rather obscure signs and Private Property, even though she was clearly on a road, she came to an imposing sign

"YOU ARE NO LONGER A TRESPASSER, YOU ARE NOW A TARGET!"

Nancy and I were at the other trailhead waiting for Judy when we received a message from Lisa "I think I'm lost!"

Nancy came to the rescue and they started texting to figure out where Lisa was and how to get to the nearest trailhead. Lisa ended up at the Chippewa Trailhead with a beautiful summation of "Looking for this trailhead is scary."

Well my friend I would have been scared too. We got the vibe that the folks on Lime Kiln Road are not very hiker friendly.

Before heading out to this hike, I actually was able to switch to my non-winter pack. Since this was my first winter of serious White Mountain Hiking, this never felt so liberating! Though, I do know that I may have to go back if attempting any higher peaks before July. Yes, The White Mountains can still get winter weather well into June.

After getting to the trailhead to start a van pulled up on the street and after Lisa's story about getting the bejesus scared out of her we were starting to feel a bit uneasy. Until the woman got out of the car and said she was waiting for a friend to hike up with her kids to the kilns and if we knew if they could do it if their friend didn't show. Nancy helped give directions and we got our first selfie of the day, you know, just to prove we did it.

We decided to take the side trail up to the Lime Kilns. Of course, the trail if you forget to turn to go to the kilns, then you end up on private property. Since we didn't want to get arrested or shot, we sure made sure we took the correct trail. The first set of kilns looked more like caves and some got nervous that a bear would emerge as we were taking pictures, so we didn't linger. Then we got to the BIG kiln. We worked really hard to hold it up since it looked like it was gonna come down any minute. We did good and saved the day. Whew...

Then a few of us took the windy staircase to the top. Now, at the top of the staircase, if one is brave, they can clamber up atop the kilns. This is not a feat for the faint of heart. Mind you, it's a giant brick structure with a large chimney in the center.

Lisa went up to the right. Made her way past the chimney, avoiding the 50 foot hole. She went up to the front to look over the edge and Nancy, who volunteered to be our photographer got some nice pictures of those of us that climbed up to the top of the chimney. While Judy went up the left side and made her way past a sapling, then made her way to the front edge. I could see that she was a bit nervous, so I got up and moved the sapling out of her way, and gave her my hand to hold as she came back through. As she was going past she spun around and I ended up getting smacked in the face (by the sapling not by Judy). I tell ya, sometimes it doesn't pay to be a good Samaritan. :-D

After our little side trip, we headed back to the main trail. All of a sudden one of our party exclaimed "Oh, Lime Kiln Road! I get it!"

This launched us into a fit of laughter.

It was kind of strange bare booting it, but we delighted in being able to actually talk to one another. While walking through the trees we had some kaleidoscope moments. All we needed to do was look up at the picture-perfect blue sky.

We were all having great conversation and enjoying the peace and quiet, well until the first of us emerged from the woods onto the first set of ledges. The peace was ripped apart by the vicious attack dogs, at least that was how it sounded by myself pulling up the rear. It turned out that there were two dogs, both were leashed so there was no actual confrontation. Only one of them was spastic, while the other just looked at us like, "it's not me, really, I love people."

The poor pups were escorted out of sight and the peace returned. We noted the remaining evidence of the old fire towers as we stepped onto the colorful ledges. It was as if we were upon a solidified ice-cream haven. A heavenly vanilla sundae with swirling chocolate and caramel sauce.

We all ventured to the far end of the ledges and were rewarded with some spectacular views. Mount Moosilauke was upfront and took center stage, even if the summit was obscured by the clouds. The clouds themselves put on an amazing display.

It was easy to forget that we hadn't yet summitted. So a little more up with just a tad bit of ice and we made it. More of the same lovely views. Then we headed back down. I don't think I've walked on a softer footed trail in New Hampshire. It was like a walk in the park and seemingly not steep at all. The elevation difference seemed so much less than from where we came. It turned out to be only about 300' difference. Just goes to show that the terrain can make all the difference.

There was one water crossing on the way out. The ladies showed their balancing skills by traversing a felled tree. While I have no grace, I rock hopped across and we all ended up staying dry, which was a small miracle.

Before we knew it, we were done. We were talking about who was going to shuttle Nancy and Lisa back to their vehicles, I walked over to the rental car and pushed the door button, to no avail. Only then did it occur to me that I'd left my keys in Nancy's car. Well, that decided who was doing the driving. And poor Nancy was elected to bring me back to car.

As we were on our way out and ducking our heads as we drove under a fallen tree across the road, we noticed all of the POSTED signs and truly understood Lisa's distress earlier that morning. All the signs were in RED and YELLOW, and on just about EVERY tree. Then we passed the road that Lisa's GPS took her down and there were indeed many obscure and rambling signs about being private property, even though the road sign was definitely not a private road. We weren't curious enough to go where Lisa had been sent. Maybe her GPS just doesn't like her...

Notable Nancyism – So much story fodder in one little hike!

OH, THE PEOPLE I'VE MET
AND AN AWARDS CEREMONY

As I reflect upon the wonderful people I've met, I am amazed, and though I'm not more than half way through any of my "lists". These characters who are bigger than life, yet all have the same feeling of humility brought about by the journey in the Whites that help us realize how small we are and what a privilege it is to experience their grandeur. Yes, The White Mountains of New Hampshire aren't the biggest or the baddest, but they are pretty spectacular in their own right. Those that appreciate this, are my people, thank you for showing up and especially thanks to those that have reached out to share their experiences.

The AMC Awards Ceremony was approaching, and Nancy suggested that we go to support our Hiking Buddies. Every April the AMC recognizes completion of one or all of four lists. The lists include, The White Mountain Four Thousand Footers, The New England Four Thousand Footers, The New England Hundred Highest, and The Northeast 111 Club.

While neither of us was up for an award in 2023, we had many friends and those we've followed from FB postings, up for receiving awards. So, Nancy and I decided we'd provide the cheering section for those we knew and those we knew of.

Stacy invited us to join her and a few other Hiking Buddies celebrants for dinner before the awards ceremony. It was so much fun meeting those we'd FB stalked and bantered with on-line in the flesh and blood. Yes, Dave Vroom is just as funny in person as he appears online. His wife, Sally, was a pleasure to chat with. The festivities had begun.

Dinner was a blast. I "hopped" up on a chair to get a selfie with everyone at the table. While up there Dave dared me to do a little dance, so I did. No, I wasn't drinking. I just enjoyed being in the moment and meeting new friends with the same screws loose.

We headed over to the Exeter High School where the ceremony was held. It felt like a night with a star studded cast of characters. Nancy and I made our way to the auditorium and found some seats. While Nancy went back to her car for her sweater I was charged with watching her belongings. Being somewhat distracted as I can be, I completely failed in my duty as I was awe stricken by all the amazing people milling about. Across the room, I spotted the group that we'd dined with and hastily made my way to where they were, leaving Nancy's bag behind. I did keep my eye out for Nancy though so she didn't head back over to our original seats. When she came back in and realized I'd failed my mission we both headed straight over to where we were, and thankfully her possessions were in tact where they were abandoned while under my care.

She was much more forgiving than I'm sure I would have been in her shoes. We headed back to the group to set up our cheering squad and picked up a couple Hiking Buddies along the way.

I brought a full complement of dollar store noise making devices and pom-poms to enhance our cheering capabilities. We blew horns, clapped our hands, cheered and shook our booties, I mean pom-poms, for everyone we knew. And everyone we didn't know for that matter.

I was in awe of all those accomplishments. They had the oldest four season 48 finisher and the youngest 48 finisher who not only finished her 48 but did so as a single season winter finisher.

Tom, whom I had met at the summit of Owl's Head, was in the audience but hadn't finished his application in time to be recognized.

I will never be the fastest or accomplish the most, but I am excited to share the stage with all the Mountain Gods. Perhaps in 2025?

Hope to see you out and about!

TRAIL ETIQUETTE

Don't be a Dick!

RESOURCES, RECOMMENDATIONS, ACRONYMS, AND DEFINITIONS

I definitely don't travel this journey alone. I have a lot of help from my friends, books, the internet, apps, and any source of support I can find. Therefore, I've compiled some resources, recommended readings, list of acronyms, and definitions as I've come to interpret them. The opinions expressed are strictly my own and as such are absolutely subjective.

Resources that I have found helpful are as follows, but are not limited to…

- The 4000-Footers of the White Mountains: A Guide and History, by Steven D. Smith and Mike Dickerman, 3rd edition, dated 2023
  - Easily my favorite resource when planning on hiking a NH 4000-Footer

- Not only does this guide provide recommended routes but provides great detail as to what to expect (i.e. water crossings, rock scrambles, when trail goes above tree line, etc.)
- AllTrails App
  - I mostly use now for directions to the trailhead
  - It did save me on my first solo hike up Mount Cardigan as described in "FIRST SOLO HIKE IN THE WHITES" chapter
- Alpine Quest App is what I use while on trail to make sure that I am still on trail
- AMC Trails Desk phone number 603-466-2721
  - Provides up to date trail conditions throughout The White Mountains
  - A live person answers so can actually interact with someone, refreshing!!
- AMC White Mountain Guide: AMCs Comprehensive Guide to Hiking Trails in the White Mountain National Forest, by Ken MacGray and Steven D. Smith, 31st edition, dated October 24, 2022
  - In addition to using the guide, it's also nice to visit Steve Smith at The Mountain Wanderer Book & Maps store in Lincoln, NH
  - Essential if planning on tracing all the AMC White Mountain Trails
- New Hampshire's 52 WITH A VIEW A Hiker's Guide, by Ken MacGray, Second edition, dated June 15, 2020
- New Hampshire & Maine White Mountains Waterproof Trail Map, by Steve Bushey and Angela Faeth, 6th edition, dated 2019
- Rangers at Stations or meet in the parking lot
- Strangers I pass or rather those that pass me on the trails
- www.amc4000footer.org

- · The official 4000 Footer list
  · Qualifications for Awards Certificates
- www.mountain-forecast.com
  - · A great source for summit forecast
  - · This is what I use for general planning purposes
- www.mountwashington.org
  - · The best short term forecast for higher summits
  - · Especially prudent when planning to hike the Northern Presidentials
- www.yosemite.org is where I booked my guided tours when I visited Yosemite National Park
- Yosemite – The Complete Guide, by James Kaiser
- FB Pages – Ah, now here are places that can be both, a blessing and a curse. Well, people are left to their own devices and can sometime run amuck. There is a lot of helpful information on these pages. There are often a lot of overlapping members on these pages, which I personally love. Most members are positive and want to help others succeed. As on all social media the occasional troll finds their way through and hopefully they don't turn you off before you get hooked on an adventure of a lifetime.
  - · The 4,000 Footer Club-Climbing and Hiking in New Hampshire
  - · Hike the 4000 footers of NH!
  - · Hikerbabes – there are local chapters as well as the general pages
  - · Hiking Buddies NH48
  - · NH 52 With A View

Recommended Reading for all 4000 Footer hikers

- Where You'll Find Me – Risk, Decisions, and the Last Climb of Kate Matrosova – by Ty Gagne
- The Last Traverse – by Ty Gagne
- Article Ty Gagne wrote that was turned into a movie, with some artistic license from what I understand, haven't seen the move, loved the article
- OK – anything written by Ty Gagne
- Desperate Steps – Life, Death, and Choices Made in the Mountains of the Northeast – by Peter W. Kick
- Following Atticus – Forty-Eight High Peaks, One Little Dog, and an Extraordinary Friendship – by Tom Ryan
- Not Without Peril – 150 Years of Misadventure on the Presidential Range of New Hampshire – by Nicholas Howe
- The White Mountain – by Dan Szczesny
- Backwoods Ethics – by Laura and Guy Waterman
- All of the Ken Bosse books

List of Acronyms
- 52WAV – 52 With A View
- AMC – Appalachian Mountain Club
- DD – Dorky Dad
- DESIREE – Driving Estimated Information Reliable Enough Entity
- EMS – Eastern Mountain Sports
- GOSA – Groton Open Space Association
- LNT – Leave No Trace
- SSW – Single Season Winter accomplishment of all NH 48 4000 Footers between winter solstice and spring equinox

- ZBOND – Zealand along with the Bonds Traverse
- Words and definitions you won't likely find in the dictionary or if you do, well, this is an interpretation more conducive to the content of this book.
- 48 – 4000 Footers – "The List" of mountains over 4,000 feet in New Hampshire as listed by the AMC that started my obsession and ultimately transformed this mild manner engineer into a Wild Woman Adventurer
- 48 over 70 – Completing all NH 48 – 4000 Footers over the age of 70. Not for the faint of heart and the patch is the coolest...
- 52WAV – Another awesome list with mountains that have a view, at least they did when the list was created
- Cairn – piles of rocks used as trail markers above treeline. These are sometimes used to mark mountain summits
- Grid – An unimaginable accomplishment of hiking EVERY 4000 Footer in Each Month, not necessarily in the same year. But some gridiots have actually accomplished this crazy feat in a single year.
- Gridiot – term of endearment with the hiking community for those that take on the Grid.
- Hister – hiking sister
- In-Tents – Supposed to be a glamping situation where one shows up and has a fully furnished tent giving an outdoor experience in comfort. Then, there was the place we stayed near Olympic National Park, Air BNBer, beware...
- Leave No Trace – Take only pictures leave only footprints
- Monorail – there's a whole section devoted to this definition in the xx chapter
- Post-holing or post-holer – intentional or unintentional holes made in snow

- Rabbitat – habitat created just for the long eared loppers
- Shoulder season – all seasons experienced in one hike
- Socked In – the mountains are essentially swallowed up by the clouds. Not only are there no views, sometimes one can't even see the trail ahead of them or where the next marker or cairn is.
- Tortoise Pace – in the hiking world people talk about pace and try to name appropriately. This would imply a turtle like pace, which is typically 1 mph or less. I personally like using tortoise because they are usually larger that turtles and take even more effort to aoul themselves and their masses on their backs up and on their feet in order to then effortfully begin ascending a mountain.
- Tramily – trail family they are not just people you meet on the tril but that you connect on a profound level connected by this shared passion.
- Tree-hugger – used to help us up mountains or off our butts

www.ingramcontent.com/pod-product-compliance
Lightning Source LLC
Chambersburg PA
CBHW071148130626
46553CB00004B/1568